H

Hannah Arendt's work offers a powerful critical engagement with the cultural and philosophical crises of mid-twentieth-century Europe. Her idea of the banality of evil, made famous after her report on the trial of the Nazi war criminal, Adolf Eichmann, remains controversial to this day.

In the face of 9/11 and the 'war on terror', Arendt's work on the politics of freedom and the rights of man in a democratic state are especially relevant. Her impassioned plea for the creation of a public sphere through free, critical thinking and dialogue provides a significant resource for contemporary thought.

Covering her key ideas from *The Origins of Totalitarianism* and *The Human Condition* as well as some of her less well-known texts, and focussing in detail on Arendt's idea of storytelling, this guide brings Arendt's work into the twenty-first century while helping students to understand its urgent relevance for the contemporary world.

Simon Swift is Lecturer in Critical and Cultural Theory in the School of English at the University of Leeds. His research interests include Kant, Romanticism, aesthetics, the philosophy of the Enlightenment and Critical Theory. He is the author of *Romanticism, Literature and Philosophy: Expressive Rationality in Rousseau, Kant, Wollstonecraft and Contemporary Theory* (2006).

ROUTLEDGE CRITICAL THINKERS

Series Editor: Robert Eaglestone, Royal Holloway, University of London

Routledge Critical Thinkers is a series of accessible introductions to key figures in contemporary critical thought.

With a unique focus on historical and intellectual contexts, the volumes in this series examine important theorists':

- significance
- motivation
- key ideas and their sources
- impact on other thinkers.

Concluding with extensively annotated guides to further reading, *Routledge Critical Thinkers* are the student's passport to today's most exciting critical thought.

Already available:

For further details on this series, see www.routledge.com/literature/series.asp

HANNAH ARENDT

Simon Swift

Routledge
Taylor & Francis Group

LONDON AND NEW YORK

First published 2009
by Routledge
2 Park Square, Milton Park, Abingdon, Oxon OX14 4RN

Simultaneously published in the USA and Canada
by Routledge
270 Madison Avenue, New York, NY 10016

Routledge is an imprint of the Taylor & Francis Group, an informa business

© 2009 Simon Swift

Typeset in Perpetua by Taylor & Francis Books
Printed and bound in Great Britain by
TJ International Ltd, Padstow, Cornwall

British Library Cataloguing in Publication Data
A catalogue record for this book is available from the British Library

Library of Congress Cataloging-in-Publication Data
Swift, Simon.
  Hannah Arendt / Simon Swift.
    p. cm. – (Routledge critical thinkers)
  Includes bibliographical references and index.
  1906-1975. I. Title. II. Series.
  B945.A694S95 2008
  320.5092–dc22

                                        2008015953

ISBN 10: 0-415-42585-9   ISBN 13: 978-0-415-42585-8 (hbk)
ISBN 10: 0-415-42586-7   ISBN 13: 978-0-415-42586-5 (pbk)
ISBN 10: 0-203-88967-3   ISBN 13: 978-0-203-88967-1 (ebk)

FOR LENI

CONTENTS

SERIES EDITOR'S PREFACE

The books in this series offer introductions to major critical thinkers who have influenced literary studies and the humanities. The *Routledge Critical Thinkers* series provides the books you can turn to first when a new name or concept appears in your studies.

Each book will equip you to approach a key thinker's original texts by explaining her or his key ideas, putting them into context and, perhaps most importantly, showing you why this thinker is considered to be significant. The emphasis is on concise, clearly written guides which do not presuppose a specialist knowledge. Although the focus is on particular figures, the series stresses that no critical thinker ever existed in a vacuum but, instead, emerged from a broader intellectual, cultural and social history. Finally, these books will act as a bridge between you and the thinker's original texts: not replacing them but rather complementing what she or he wrote.

These books are necessary for a number of reasons. In his 1997 autobiography, *Not Entitled*, the literary critic Frank Kermode wrote of a time in the 1960s:

> On beautiful summer lawns, young people lay together all night, recovering from their daytime exertions and listening to a troupe of Balinese musicians. Under their blankets or their sleeping bags, they would chat drowsily about the gurus of the time ... What they repeated was largely hearsay; hence my

There is still a need for 'authoritative and intelligible introductions'.
But this series reflects a different world from the 1960s. New thinkers
have emerged and the reputations of others have risen and fallen, as
new research has developed. New methodologies and challenging ideas
have spread through the arts and humanities. The study of literature is
no longer – if it ever was – simply the study and evaluation of poems,
novels and plays. It is also the study of the ideas, issues and difficulties
which arise in any literary text and in its interpretation. Other arts
and humanities subjects have changed in analogous ways.

With these changes, new problems have emerged. The ideas and
issues behind these radical changes in the humanities are often presented without reference to wider contexts or as theories which you
can simply 'add on' to the texts you read. Certainly, there's nothing
wrong with picking out selected ideas or using what comes to hand –
indeed, some thinkers have argued that this is, in fact, all we can do.
However, it is sometimes forgotten that each new idea comes from
the pattern and development of somebody's thought and it is important to study the range and context of their ideas. Against theories
'floating in space', the *Routledge Critical Thinkers* series places key
thinkers and their ideas firmly back in their contexts.

More than this, these books reflect the need to go back to the
thinker's own texts and ideas. Every interpretation of an idea, even the
most seemingly innocent one, offers its own 'spin', implicitly or expli-
citly. To read only books on a thinker, rather than texts by that thinker, is to deny yourself a chance of making up your own mind.
Sometimes what makes a significant figure's work hard to approach is
not so much its style or content as the feeling of not knowing where
to start. The purpose of these books is to give you a 'way in' by
offering an accessible overview of these thinkers' ideas and works and
by guiding your further reading, starting with each thinker's own
texts. To use a metaphor from the philosopher Ludwig Wittgenstein
(1889–1951), these books are ladders, to be thrown away after you
have climbed to the next level. Not only, then, do they equip you to
approach new ideas, but also they empower you, by leading you back
to a theorist's own texts and encouraging you to develop your own
informed opinions.

Finally, these books are necessary because, just as intellectual needs have changed, the education systems around the world – the contexts in which introductory books are usually read – have changed radically, too. What was suitable for the minority higher education system of the 1960s is not suitable for the larger, wider, more diverse, high-technology education systems of the twenty-first century. These changes call not just for new, up-to-date introductions but new methods of presentation. The presentational aspects of *Routledge Critical Thinkers* have been developed with today's students in mind.

Each book in the series has a similar structure. They begin with a section offering an overview of the life and ideas of each thinker and explain why she or he is important. The central section of each book discusses the thinker's key ideas, their context, evolution and reception. Each book concludes with a survey of the thinker's impact, outlining how their ideas have been taken up and developed by others. In addition, there is a detailed final section suggesting and describing books for further reading. This is not a 'tacked-on' section but an integral part of each volume. In the first part of this section you will find brief descriptions of the thinker's key works, then, following this, information on the most useful critical works and, in some cases, on relevant websites. This section will guide you in your reading, enabling you to follow your interests and develop your own projects. Throughout each book, references are given in what is known as the Harvard system (the author and the date of a work cited are given in the text and you can look up the full details in the bibliography at the back). This offers a lot of information in very little space. The books also explain technical terms and use boxes to describe events or ideas in more detail, away from the main emphasis of the discussion. Boxes are also used at times to highlight definitions of terms frequently used or coined by a thinker. In this way, the boxes serve as a kind of glossary, easily identified when flicking through the book.

The thinkers in the series are 'critical' for three reasons. First, they are examined in the light of subjects which involve criticism: principally literary studies or English and cultural studies, but also other disciplines which rely on the criticism of books, ideas, theories and unquestioned assumptions. Second, they are critical because studying their work will provide you with a 'toolkit' for your own informed critical reading and thought, which will make you critical. Third, these thinkers are critical because they are crucially important: they deal with ideas and questions which can overturn conventional under-standings of the world, of texts, of everything we take for granted, leaving us with a deeper understanding of what we already knew and with new ideas.

No introduction can tell you everything. However, by offering a way into critical thinking, this series hopes to begin to engage you in an activity which is productive, constructive and potentially life-changing.

ACKNOWLEDGEMENTS

I want to thank Bob Eaglestone for his enthusiasm for this project from the start, and Aileen Storry, Development Editor for Cultural Studies at Routledge, for her patience throughout the composition. I'd also like to thank the School of English at Leeds for granting the study leave that enabled me to finish this book. Friends and colleagues in the School who have inspired me throughout its composition are Bridget Bennet, Sam Durrant and Denis Flannery. This book would not have been possible without the love and support of Heike.

ABBREVIATIONS

Full bibliographic references to the following texts published by Arendt, and posthumously published works, can be found in the 'Works cited' section.

BPF	*Between Past and Future: Eight Exercises in Political Thought*
CR	*Crises of the Republic*
EJ	*Eichmann in Jerusalem: A Report on the Banality of Evil*
EU	*Essays in Understanding 1930–1954: Formation, Exile and Totalitarianism*
HC	*The Human Condition*
JW	*The Jewish Writings*
LKPP	*Lectures on Kant's Political Philosophy*
LM	*The Life of the Mind*
MDT	*Men in Dark Times*
OR	*On Revolution*
OT1/2/3	*The Origins of Totalitarianism* (volumes 1, 2 and 3)
PP	'Philosophy and Politics'
RV	*Rahel Varnhagen: The Life of a Jewess*

WHY ARENDT?

Hannah Arendt (1906–75) is a crucial thinker for anyone who wants to make sense of the traumatic story of twentieth-century European history, and who believes more generally that it is the purpose of thinking to illuminate the world around us. She is an acknowledged figure in the fields of political theory, philosophy, modern history and cultural studies, and she is also a guiding spirit for the emerging fields of holocaust studies and Jewish studies. Alongside its elucidation of Arendt's key political and philosophical ideas, a central purpose of this book will be to claim Arendt for literary studies. It will consider the ways in which Arendt's work can help us to think about the role of literature, and in particular literary narrative, in making sense of history and of our cultural and political identity. Arendt valued storytelling over philosophical thinking for its attentiveness to the singular nature of human experience. Her work consistently challenged hegemonic and absolute notions of 'truth' by proposing a new way of understanding the relationship between the particular human self, the community in which that self is found and the wider world. Literature offered Arendt a crucial resource in undertaking this departure from the philosophical tradition. 'No philosophy', she wrote in a late essay, 'can compare in intensity and richness of meaning with a properly narrated story' (MDT: 22).

Arendt's name is probably less familiar than the names of many other critical thinkers covered by this series. Her work is rarely found on the various modules in critical and literary theory that are offered to undergraduates in literary and cultural studies. This is a shame, given the usefulness of Arendt for students of literature that this book wants to claim. The dominant conceptions of critical thinking and 'theory' in English and cultural studies have, instead, more often been tailored to fit the work of a number of thinkers, usually French and often male, who were attracting attention and causing controversy in English departments around the time of Arendt's death in 1975. Arendt is then a thinker who preceded the theory revolution, to the extent that her death coincided, more or less, with the appearance of theory in institutions of higher education in the English-speaking world.

In the last few years, this dominant idea of 'theory' has been subjected to a robust challenge. In his recent book *After Theory*, Terry Eagleton has stated this challenge in a rather tongue-in-cheek way.

> The golden age of cultural theory is long past. The pioneering works of Jacques Lacan, Claude Lévi-Strauss, Louis Althusser, Roland Barthes and Michel Foucault are several decades behind us [...] Some of them have since been struck down. Fate pushed Roland Barthes under a Parisian laundry van, and afflicted Michel Foucault with Aids. It dispatched Lacan, Williams and Bourdieu, and banished Louis Althusser to a psychiatric hospital for the murder of his wife. It seemed that God was not a structuralist.
>
> (Eagleton 2004: 1)

The fact that most of the pioneers of theory are dead is not the only reason why Eagleton thinks that our current condition is decidedly 'after theory'. To a number of contemporary commentators, including Eagleton, the ideas of these master theorists have also proved to be incapable of keeping pace with some of the drastic changes in the global situation at the beginning of the twenty-first century. In particular, these ideas seem increasingly outdated or irrelevant in the era of the 'war on terror'. For example, the eminent gender theorist Judith Butler (1949–), in her recent book *Precarious Life*, proposed an alternative frame for understanding the violence of the terrorist attacks of 11 September 2001. Rather than interpreting them as an act of war, Butler argues that we might understand the attacks on the Twin Towers and the Pentagon as evidence of 'an inevitable interdependency [...] as the basis for global political community'. In making this claim, Butler also confesses to 'not knowing how to theorise that interdependency' (Butler 2004: xii–xiii). There is an important sense in which events such as those of 9/11 seem potentially to exhaust the capacity of 'theory' or 'theorising' to make sense of them. But it is also notable that efforts such as Butler's to offer a different kind of critical response to the new fundamentalisms which increasingly seem to tyrannise over our world are importantly indebted to Arendt.

The aim of this book will be to introduce you to Arendt's key ideas by pointing out the ways in which they resonate with the cultural and political dilemmas that we face today, while also offering a clear and balanced account of how Arendt's work was conditioned by her response to the cultural, political and intellectual crises that defined her own age. Arendt was a refugee from Nazi Germany and then a stateless person for almost twenty years, as well as a Jewish intellectual with a complex and sometimes controversial attitude towards the state of Israel. She was one of the first critical thinkers to offer a sustained reflection on the horrors of the Nazi death camps and, after she became an American citizen in 1951, a public intellectual who involved herself avidly in the public life of the nation that had given her sanctuary. Arendt's own life-story then remained intimately involved with some of the key events in the political history of the twentieth century.

Arendt's life spans the first three-quarters of the last century, and at the centre of her life's work and her lived experience are found the horrors that totalitarian rule inflicted on Europe. For Arendt, what went on in Germany between 1933 and 1945 and in the Soviet Union under Stalin was without precedent. These were events that defied any form of systematic categorisation, or in other words, any attempt to understand them by subsuming them under existing political categories. Arendt thought, for example, that any attempt to understand totalitarian rule using the classical political concept of tyranny risked distorting an understanding of what was radically new and unprecedented about totalitarianism. This radical newness of the totalitarian regimes made it extraordinarily difficult for existing theoretical and philosophical systems to cope with the task of accounting for them. Like many others of her generation, Arendt then turned to art, and in particular to narrative and storytelling, in order to come to some form of preliminary understanding of the nature of the acts of the totalitarian regimes, that often seem to border on the incomprehensible.

In the words of one Arendt critic:

> Arendt herself no longer thought it either desirable or even possible to fit the world into a coherent 'philosophical *Weltanschauung*' [philosophical world view]. For her, political philosophy became a method of narration to 'cull meaning from the past,' an exercise in establishing distinctions that would enable us to think the meaning of our times and our actions, to 'think what we are doing.'
>
> (Benhabib 1996: 118)

Arendt thought that stories had the potential to offer a more attentive and particular treatment of events than philosophical and theoretical systems. She was committed to the idea that each event that happens in the world is new and unique, and that we always risk doing violence to the event's newness and uniqueness by trying to fit it into an overall world view, or by trying to impose a preformed theoretical explanation onto it. The effort to theorise an historical event, Arendt thought, often involves an attempt to categorise it alongside other earlier events, which dulls our sense of what might be new and unique about the new event. She thought that storytelling opens up the possibility of different interpretations, based on the differing world views of those who hear the story, and also the possibility of an open-ended, perhaps inconclusive debate about the meaning of the story. As Arendt wrote in an essay on the Danish writer Isak Dinesen (1885–1963), 'storytelling reveals meaning without committing the error of defining it', while 'it brings about consent and reconciliation with things as they really are' (MDT: 105).

Storytelling is particularly useful in the case of terrible and disturbing events that are difficult to comprehend or to imagine, particularly for those who have not lived through them. Storytelling can therefore be a useful tool for coping with the tragedy and the trauma of history. In the words of Isak Dinesen, as quoted by Hannah Arendt, 'All sorrows can be borne if you put them into a story or tell a story about them' (MDT: 104). But as much as it might be understood as a tool for coping with history, Arendt thought that storytelling offers an important tool for resisting the evils of the modern world.

In his memoir of his time as a prisoner in the concentration camp at Auschwitz in the last years of the Second World War, *If This Is a Man*, the Italian author Primo Levi (1919–87) remembers a conversation he had had in his first days in the camp with a fellow inmate, an ex-sergeant of the Austro-Hungarian army called Steinlauf. Levi is remembering how he had quickly given up on any attempt to keep himself clean in the squalid conditions of the camp, and how Steinlauf had upbraided him for this. As Levi remembers it, Steinlauf tells him

> that even in this place one can survive, and therefore one must want to survive, to tell the story, to bear witness: and that to survive we must force ourselves to save at least the skeleton, the scaffolding, the form of civilization. We are slaves, deprived of every right, exposed to every insult, condemned to certain death, but we still possess one power, and we must defend it with all our strength for it is the last – the power to refuse our consent. So we must certainly wash our faces in dirty water and dry ourselves on our jackets. We must polish our shoes, not because the regulation states it, but for dignity and propriety.
> (Levi 1987: 47)

What seems to Levi at first sight to be an act of conformity, a falling-in with the camp authority's insistence that the prisoners maintain an impossible standard of hygiene and decency in the most degrading of conditions, is revealed here to be a profound act of resistance. Steinlauf obeys orders, but not because they are orders; rather, because he wants to preserve his humanity. In this way, he exercises a more potent power of rebellion than giving up on washing could ever entail. He rebels against the expectation of the camp authorities that its inmates will lose their humanity.

This incident in Levi's narrative offers an important meditation on the nature of human dignity and on the relation of oppressed peoples to the authority that oppresses them. But it does so in a thoroughly particularised and embodied way. It is difficult to imagine its meaning holding the same power if it were abstracted fully from Levi's story. Perhaps even the brief reading that I have extracted from it above does violence to the story's complexity and subtlety. This passage also describes a link between storytelling and survival. Steinlauf argues that 'one must want to survive, to tell the story, to bear witness'. The need to survive Auschwitz is bound together with the need to tell the story of what happened there, to bear witness to its horror. The act of storytelling becomes, in Levi's narrative, a retrospective act of resistance to the horrifying degradations of the camp's slave economy. In other words, in telling the story of his encounter with Steinlauf, Levi is perhaps meditating on his own survival of Auschwitz. By surviving, and by telling his story, Levi has taken up Steinlauf's challenge to save 'the form of civilisation'. The fact that he has survived to tell the story could be taken to show that the attempt to destroy the humanity of this inmate of Auschwitz has failed (although I by no means would want to suggest this as a definitive reading of Levi's text; one might equally argue that civilisation was destroyed in the concentration camps, and find ways to show that Levi thought this too).

Chapters 6, 7 and 8 of this book will show how Arendt's important work *The Origins of Totalitarianism* (1951) sought to tell the story of how and why the totalitarian movements of the mid-twentieth century could have happened. Like Steinlauf, Arendt imagined this telling of the story of totalitarianism as an act of resistance. By telling the story of the origins of the totalitarian movements, Arendt's study teaches us how to recognise what was new and unprecedented about them, and what it was about them that made them defy classification or systematic understanding. Arendt's story also sought to guard against what she thought to be the very real possibility that totalitarianism might erupt once more into the post-war world. 'Comprehension', wrote Arendt in her preface to the 1967 edition of *The Origins of Totalitarianism*, 'means the unpremeditated, attentive facing up to, and resisting of, reality – whatever it may be or might have been' (OT1: x).

Arendt thought of the activity of telling stories as an exercise in political understanding. Storytelling proved to be particularly enabling in her attempt to understand events that take place at the limits of what can be understood. Telling stories is something that we do, it is an active, dynamic and creative activity, and it was often opposed by Arendt to the static intellectual models of understanding that we inherit from the idea of 'theory' in Western culture. Storytelling, as cultural anthropologists have long recognised, is also traditionally the way in which cultures order their understanding of themselves; by being put into the form of a narrative, a series of events can be understood, and so it can be communicated to a wider audience and remembered by the community. If stories help us to understand, if they make events intelligible, they also presuppose an idea of community inherent in the act of telling, which involves at once the teller of the story, the hero of the action, and the listener or reader who stands back, judges it and responds to it. In this sense, too, storytelling already describes another key idea of Arendt's thought: that free thinking is an activity that can only really go on in the presence of others, in a community, rather than in the quiet withdrawal and meditation demanded by theory.

Alongside its appreciation for storytelling, and its effort to tell stories, Arendt's work is also characterised by an attack on traditional forms of philosophical thinking and theory. A major purpose of this book, and in particular Chapters 2 and 3, will then be to examine the nature of Arendt's attack on philosophy. This attack is by no means unique to her, and Chapters 4 and 5 will examine the intellectual and historical background to the challenge that Arendt launched to the certainties and confidence of philosophical knowledge. In particular, these chapters will offer a detailed exploration of the crucial influence of two other critical thinkers on Arendt's work: the Enlightenment philosopher Immanuel Kant (1724–1804) and her contemporary Martin Heidegger (1889–1976). As well as having had a profound impact on the development of Arendt's own ideas, these were two of the key influences on the wider development of critical thinking in the twentieth century.

Part of Arendt's attack on philosophy stems from her fundamental inquiry into the nature of politics. Arendt's work is urgently political, but it claims that the whole tradition of 'theory' in the West, going right back to the work of the ancient Greek philosophers Plato (424–347 BC) and Aristotle (384–322 BC), exposes a gaping hole where real political thinking should be. Even when philosophers talk about politics, such as in Plato's blueprint for a political state in the *Republic*, Arendt claims that they are usually dismissive of the dignity and importance of the political realm. They see politics as a problem to be coped with, rather than as something which is important in its own right. Politics, which involves dialogue, persuasion and the need to recognise the claims of others, is simply, according to Arendt, too messy, opaque and human for most philosophers and theorists. It disturbs the quiet space needed by philosophical thought with the noise and uncertainty of a public realm. Many of these ideas are explored in a key book of Arendt's, *The Human Condition* (1958), which will be considered in detail in Chapters 2 and 3.

The tendency of philosophy, as Arendt saw it, to withdraw from the public realm into solitary contemplation and abstraction aroused her suspicion. In Arendt's view, this withdrawal often led philosophers to unfortunate life decisions at times of political crisis, something of which she had had first-hand experience. Martin Heidegger, who in 1924 had been Arendt's teacher and her lover, briefly became a member of the Nazi party in the early 1930s, an event that was shrouded in silence until after his death, and that remains controversial. Arendt was struck by the contrast between Heidegger's enormous philosophical subtlety, and his failure to have any insight, early on, into the real nature of the Nazi regime. Arendt wanted to understand the historical and cultural influences that made this contrast in Heidegger possible.

Arendt thought that philosophical thinking had been distorted by a tradition which has been dominant in the West for over two thousand years, that goes back to the work of Plato, and that has looked down on politics. Arendt also thought that in the modern period some philosophers, such as Kant, had managed to step outside the philosophical tradition, and she wanted to develop the possibilities opened up by their work in her own. Arendt's work sought to offer a reassessment of the philosophical tradition, and in particular to think about how its abstract theorising had inflicted violence onto the public world, and onto the activity of thinking itself, by defining it in a particularly narrow way.

Each of the following chapters will seek to 'tell the story' of Arendt's key ideas, and of her relation to other thinkers and writers. This book will then mobilise Arendt's argument about narrative as a means of understanding her own work. At the same time, it will pay close attention to Arendt's use of literary examples in her work. It will describe the ways in which she makes use of the work of writers such as Herman Melville and Joseph Conrad in order to elucidate her political ideas, and it will also think about wider connections between Arendt's ideas and literary writing in English. This will be done, in each chapter, through a case study that will interrupt the narrative of the chapter, stand back, and seek to elucidate the key idea under consideration by describing one of Arendt's readings of a literary work or by thinking about how the key idea impacts on a particular concern in literary studies. The focus throughout the book will therefore be on those aspects of Arendt's work that are likely to be of most interest to students of literature, although these are also crucial aspects of Arendt's work as a whole. A central assumption of the book will be that the disciplinary boundaries which fence in and define what it means to study literature, what it means to study philosophy and what it means to study political theory, often inhibit the creative potential that these subject areas otherwise hold. By suspending those boundaries, as Arendt did in her own work, this book will suggest that we can learn from her about how to read literary texts in dynamic and unexpected ways. Each chapter will revisit the core themes that

Arendt grappled with throughout her life – the nature of politics, the purpose of storytelling, the relation between action and thinking – and so, while readers who want to focus on particular aspects of her thought should find that each chapter stands alone, reading the chapters sequentially as an unfolding story of their own, the story of Hannah Arendt's life and work, will yield the richest understanding of her.

Finally, two brief observations about Hannah Arendt. The final section of this book will suggest some of the ways in which Arendt is becoming a crucial figure for contemporary critical thought. In many ways, this might seem to be a rather unexpected state of affairs. Arendt was notoriously hostile, for example, to the feminist movement, and whenever she discusses the human individual in her work, that individual is always described as a 'he' or as a 'man'. Arendt's relation to feminism will be discussed in the final section, but since a major aim of this book is to recover the meaning of Arendt's argument in its proper context, I have decided to echo Arendt in the main, and to use the masculine pronoun when describing the various characters and social personality types that people her work. At other points, though, when I have sought to suggest the usefulness of Arendt's work for a feminist politics, such as in my discussion of her idea of the spectator (Chapter 5) I have broken with Arendt and described these selves as 'she'.

The second observation concerns Arendt's contemporary relevance. I believe that Hannah Arendt was a critical thinker whom we need crucially. In a number of her later essays about American politics and culture, Arendt wrote about issues that remain relevant to us today, such as the nature of civil liberties, the problem of state-sponsored violence, and the culture of lying and criminality in politics since the Vietnam War. As I write this, a debate rages in the media about the execution of the former Iraqi dictator Saddam Hussein, who went to the gallows late in 2006 in controversial circumstances. Arendt was a critical thinker who was profoundly concerned with questions about personal responsibility for atrocity, with problems of international justice and crimes against humanity, as well as with philosophical questions about judgement. Ultimately, Arendt condoned a practice of judgement that took place in the bright light of public space; perhaps this idea might begin to offer us illumination once again.

1

BIOGRAPHY, THEORY AND POLITICS

This chapter will narrate some of the important events in Arendt's life-story, before introducing a number of her key ideas about politics and society. However, Arendt's ideas and her life-story (or biography) are not completely distinct concerns for this study of her. I will suggest in what follows some of the ways in which Arendt's biography and her ideas are in fact constantly intertwined. It is a key tenet of Arendt's own work that the life-story of a thinker, artist or politician provides a crucial context in which to understand his or her thought.

Before looking at Arendt's life-story, it might be worthwhile to pause and think about what is at stake in the very idea of telling the story of a critical thinker's life (something that a critical introduction to a thinker's work might very reasonably be expected to do, but that often, in practice, is done with a degree of reluctance by the authors of such introductions). A preoccupation with (auto)biography has, since Arendt's death, become rather unfashionable. More recent critical thought has suggested that a focus on the biography of an author or thinker can in fact distract from a rigorous reading of their texts. Arendt's teacher Martin Heidegger once claimed that the biography of the ancient Greek philosopher Aristotle could be summed up in a single sentence: he was born, he thought, he died. Everything else, according to Heidegger, is mere anecdote. Heidegger's hostility to biography has had a particularly powerful impact on literary theory in the last thirty or so years, as it has sought to liberate literary critics from a dependence on the biography of the author as the source of an authoritative account of the meaning of a literary text. As the semiologist and cultural critic Roland Barthes (1915–80) wrote in 1967 in his essay 'The Death of the Author':

> The *author* still reigns in histories of literature, biographies of writers, interviews, magazines, as in the very consciousness of men of letters anxious to unite their person and their work through diaries and memoirs. The image of literature to be found in ordinary culture is tyrannically centred on the author, his person, his life, his tastes, his passions […] The *explanation* of a work is always sought in the man or woman who produced it, as if it were always in the end, through the more or less transparent allegory of the fiction, the voice of a single person, of the *author* 'confiding' in us.
>
> (Barthes 2001: 1466)

Barthes was struck, in his essay, by the reader's desire for an intimate relationship with the author. He thought of the biography industry as a symptom of the modern reader's desire to seek out in the author's life-story something personal or hidden, such as his tastes or his passions, and to define this intimate knowledge as the real source of meaning in the author's writing. For Barthes, the belief that we can gain intimate knowledge of the author's inner life is in fact an illusion, the product of a trick that is played on the reader by consumer capitalism. Barthes argued that in capitalistic modernity, literary texts have been turned into commodities. The text-as-commodity plays its trick by suggesting to the reader that the author has singled him out, that the author confides the secret, intimate meaning of his life to that reader alone and to no-one else. Barthes wanted to shatter this illusory, narcissistic relationship between reader and writing by claiming that the author is just another fiction that has been invented by a capitalist system that wants to attribute ownership to all commodities, literary texts among them.

While these ideas might make Hannah Arendt seem, at first glance, to be retrograde and unfashionable, in fact she shared her generation's suspicion of the biography industry. Like Barthes, she was suspicious of the cult of individuality that sought to attribute all meaning to the single consciousness of an author. For her, stories are always the work of a community, and the teller of the story is no more the 'owner' of its meaning than the audience, or the hero of the story itself. She also shared Barthes's critical attitude towards the reader's desire for intimacy with the author. Throughout her life, she remained suspicious of the desire to pry into an author's private life that typifies the work of biography as Barthes describes it. In her essay on the writer Isak Dinesen, Arendt wrote:

> The connection of an artist's life with his work has always raised embarrassing problems, and our eagerness to see recorded, displayed, and discussed in public what were once strictly private affairs and nobody's business is probably less legitimate than our curiosity is ready to admit.

(MDT: 98)

The key words here are 'public' and 'private'. There is a certain zone in the life of any human being, the zone of 'intimacy' or the private world that should never, for Arendt, appear in public, and only ever does so with dire consequences. This separation of public and private spheres is a key idea in her thought as a whole.

A healthy scepticism about biography does not mean that we must abandon any interest in the life of a thinker, Arendt's included. Arendt wanted to imagine a different kind of biography, a different kind of life-story, from the one that Barthes attacks. She was, in particular, committed to the idea of a life lived in public, which can and indeed must be recorded in order to grasp the ways in which a thinker's thought is conditioned by and conditions the world around them. This chapter will now narrate the story of Arendt's own life, and in particular the story of her effort to live her life in public and the problems that she encountered in trying to do this, before introducing in a more precise way what is at stake in her distinction between 'public' and 'private' lives.

ARENDT'S LIFE-STORY

Arendt was born in the German city of Hannover in 1906, to an assimilated Jewish family, and brought up mainly in the east Prussian city of Königsberg, now part of Russia. She recalled in a television interview in 1964 that 'the word "Jew" was never mentioned at home. I first encountered it [...] in the anti-Semitic remarks of children as we played in the streets' (Young-Bruehl 2004: 11). As Arendt remembers it, 'Jew' was an identity that was imposed onto her from the outside, a label given to her, as a child, by non-Jewish children. 'Jew' was, from the start, an identity that in some way 'belonged' to anti-Semites, a label that was put on to assimilated Jews who did not necessarily recognise themselves in it. Arendt's relation to her Jewishness, and her understanding of the social status of Jews in European society, is a complex and important issue that informed her treatment of totalitarianism (see Chapter 6).

Arendt studied at the universities of Heidelberg and Marburg, where she came under the influence of perhaps the most powerful intellectual presence of her life, the philosopher Martin Heidegger, who supervised the early stages of her doctoral work on the medieval theologian and philosopher St Augustine (354–430). Heidegger was himself the student of another crucial figure in the history of the development of critical thought, Edmund Husserl (1859–1938), who had pioneered the philosophical method known as phenomenology. Although Heidegger, at the time of his first contact with Hannah Arendt, was breaking away from Husserl's influence and plotting new and uncharted territory in his thinking as he worked towards the publication of his book *Being and Time* (1927), the phenomenological revolution is a crucial background both for his and for Arendt's thought.

PHENOMENOLOGY

Phenomenology might be compared to psychoanalysis, and Husserl's work might be compared to that of Sigmund Freud (1856–1939), as two pioneering attempts to offer scientific accounts of human consciousness. But where psychoanalysis was preoccupied with offering an account of the relation between the conscious and unconscious mind, phenomenology became preoccupied with the attempt to offer a scientific account of how we see things in the world. This involved the phenomenologist in the act of 'digging down' in an attempt to unearth the fundamental structures of human consciousness that determine the nature of perception. In the process, phenomenology was able to offer a radically strange and unfamiliar account of everyday experience. One of the key interests of phenomenology is in how human beings experience time, and what relation time has to their perception of the world. In the work of Heidegger, and then in the work of Arendt, Husserl's ideas were applied to questions about culture and history, and in particular to core human experiences such as birth, death and the experience of art. Phenomenology made possible an exhilarating suspension of our fundamental and habitual ways of understanding ourselves, the world around us and the relation between the two. In Heidegger's words, 'At bottom, the ordinary is not ordinary; it is extraordinary' (Heidegger 1993: 179).

After Hitler became the chancellor of Germany in 1933, Arendt was briefly detained by the German authorities for gathering information, on behalf of the German Zionist Organisation, about how anti-Semitism was becoming official German policy. She felt compelled to leave Germany, first for France, where she worked for a Jewish refugee agency in Paris that was helping Jewish children and young people to make their way to Palestine, before being briefly interned in a concentration camp at Gurs at the foot of the Pyrenees after the German invasion of France in the summer of 1940. She ultimately made her escape to the USA in 1941. America would remain her home for the rest of her life.

It is possible to date Arendt's loss of faith in traditional philosophy and its institutions from the time of Hitler's rise to power. To this extent, but also in other ways, it became the key and defining event in her life as a public figure. Her brief experience of life in Nazi Germany was important to her intellectual development because it had presented Arendt with a shocking realisation about the unwillingness of German intellectuals to resist Nazi rule. As she recalled in an interview in 1964:

Many people think these days that the shock undergone by the Jews in 1933 was a function of Hitler's seizing power. As far as I and those of my generation are concerned, this is a curious misunderstanding. That was, of course, terrible. But it was political, it wasn't personal [...] the general political realities transformed themselves into personal destiny as soon as you set foot outside of the house [...] I lived in an intellectual milieu, but I also knew many people who did not, and I came to the conclusion that cooperation was, so to speak, the rule among intellectuals, but not among others. And I have never forgotten that. I left Germany guided by the resolution – a very exaggerated one – that 'Never again!' I will never have anything to do with 'the history of ideas' again. I didn't, indeed, want to have anything to do with this sort of society again.

(Cited in Young-Bruehl 2004: 108)

A key aspect of Arendt's effort to understand the period of totalitarian rule is her challenge to certain lazy assumptions about the nature of totalitarianism that were forming and solidifying very quickly in the years after the victory over Nazi Germany. What was shocking for her about this period was not the 'political' fact of Hitler's rise to power, which had seemed inevitable for several years anyway, but the personal shock of how the German intellectual class, many of them friends and acquaintances, had cooperated with the new regime. Once again, her work is governed by an awareness of the distinction between the public and the private, the political and the personal. Arendt wants to maintain an awareness of this distinction, but she is also aware of how the two can easily become entangled in a particular life-story.

Perhaps the most famous – or infamous – example of the cooperation that Arendt describes here came when Heidegger was appointed rector of Freiburg University in the spring of 1933, after his predecessor was dismissed for refusing to cooperate with the new official policy of excluding Jewish academic staff. In a speech given as the new rector, Heidegger famously referred to 'the greatness, the nobility of this national awakening', effectively condoning the Nazi rise to power (cited in Young-Bruehl 2004: 108). (It must be noted that Heidegger quickly became aware that he had been misled in his support for the Nazis.) Arendt was struck, in her brief experience of Nazi rule, by how intellectuals, those committed to the life of the mind, seemed incapable of seeing through the Nazi regime in the heady, exciting days of the early 1930s. For Arendt, this awareness of the naivety of intellectuals in relation to the public world became a defining insight.

Arendt's vow to abandon the world of ideas in 1933 was, as she says, exaggerated. But even so, she never became a permanent member of a university faculty in North America. For much of her life in America she remained a kind of freelance journalist and social and political thinker. From 1944, she took on a role directing research for the Commission of Jewish Cultural Reconstruction, a role that took her back to Europe after the war, and back into contact with Heidegger. Arendt also took on various roles as a visiting professor at institutions of higher education such as the New School for Social Research in New York and the Committee on Social Thought at Chicago University, and she was the first woman at Princeton University to become a professor. But Arendt remained, to borrow a phrase from the feminist thinker Gayatri Spivak (1942–), 'outside in the teaching machine'. This perhaps shows her distrust for traditional methods of thinking and its institutions, as well as her desire to carve out a new, independent role for the intellectual in public culture. No doubt this was partly informed by Arendt's experience of the depressing way in which many faculty members in German universities had shown little resistance to Hitler's rise to power in the 1930s, and scant support for their Jewish colleagues who were banned from teaching.

Arendt's life in America eventually saw her participating actively in American public life and its debates in the 1950s and 1960s about civil rights, civil disobedience and racial segregation, political corruption and the Vietnam War. In the first years after her arrival in America, though, when the war in Europe was still raging, Arendt took a strong and active role in the Zionist movement, urging the formation of a Jewish army to fight Hitler in her contributions to a German language newspaper published by the Jewish émigré community, *Aufbau*. Arendt was profoundly resistant to a view of the Jews as innocent victims of the Nazis, a view that she thought the Jews of Europe had taken on about themselves, and that she also thought was very damaging to their self-understanding and their political identity. She wanted to claim, instead, that Jews needed to take responsibility for their actions, rather than simply portraying themselves as innocent victims, or 'lambs to the slaughter'. Joining the fight against Hitler as a unified Jewish force, thought Arendt, would mean that they took control of their destiny. The formation of a Jewish army might mean, she suggested in the title to one of her articles, 'the beginning of Jewish politics'.

Arendt was profoundly suspicious of any attempt to understand Jews as innocent 'scapegoats' for Germany's problems, another assumption about totalitarian rule that she wanted to demystify. She nevertheless thought that this was a highly seductive interpretation of what had happened to them under Nazi rule. There is, she writes at the beginning of *The Origins of Totalitarianism*:

> a temptation to return to an explanation which automatically discharges the victim of responsibility: it seems quite adequate to a reality in which nothing strikes us more forcefully than the utter innocence of the individual caught in the horror machine and his utter inability to change his fate.

(OT1: 6)

Arendt's claim led her to a rather uncomfortable conclusion. If Jews were not innocent victims of Nazi violence, then in some measure they shared responsibility for that violence. This responsibility of the victims of violence needs to be faced and understood if the dignity of the victims, their status as public actors, is to be restored.

Arendt's arguments about Jewish freedom and responsibility proved to be, and indeed remain, highly controversial. Her fame and notoriety in America were ultimately guaranteed by an event that brought about a definitive break with Zionism on precisely this issue of the responsibility of the victim. In 1961, Arendt filed a series of reports from Israel for *New Yorker* magazine on the trial of Adolf Eichmann, a Nazi war criminal involved in the organisation of the Final Solution who had been kidnapped in Argentina by the Israeli secret service and put on trial in Jerusalem. Arendt's response to the trial offended much of Jewish and, particularly, Zionist public opinion by appearing to suggest that the leadership of the Jewish communities in Eastern Europe during the Second World War bore partial responsibility for the annihilation of their communities. In a brief passage of the book that she developed from her reports, *Eichmann in Jerusalem: A Report on the Banality of Evil* (1963), Arendt described how the leadership co-operated with the Nazi transportations of Jews to the east, and asked why it was that this leadership didn't resist or at least make more difficult the administration of the transportations. In this book Arendt also opened up awkward questions about how we set about judging the criminality of the Holocaust according to established legal and moral norms, and in particular about the difficulties of attributing moral responsibility for such a terrible event to bureaucrats such as Eichmann. The accused, who was responsible for organising transportation of Jews to the concentration camps, and who claimed in the trial never to have been directly involved in the killing itself, emerges as a rather pathetic and deluded figure in Arendt's account of him. To many of Arendt's observers, her telling of the story of the trial, and of Eichmann's own life-story, seemed to reserve for him sympathy which should more appropriately have been directed towards those who suffered as a result of his actions.

The Eichmann trial was a crucial episode in Arendt's life-story. The controversy that arose from her account of it became in some ways the defining event in her formation as a public intellectual, by forcing her to put off books that she had planned to write, and to devote her time and energy to justifying her position. The Eichmann controversy shows how events in the public world can shape the ideas of a thinker.

ARENDT AND THEORY

What kind of a critical thinker was Hannah Arendt? It may at first encounter seem to be excessively difficult to fit her work into an overall genealogy of critical thought. While Arendt was indebted to the work of several key thinkers who have also had an influence on later theoretical writing, particularly Martin Heidegger, Karl Marx (1818–83) and Friedrich Nietzsche (1844–1900), she makes use of them in a very different way from later post-structuralist and postmodern thinkers. Arendt produced work that is hard to categorise, and that goes out of its way to explode any settled definition of what 'theorising' might mean. For example, at times she was very hostile to Marxism, but she was also respectful of the internal consistency of Marx's work, and of the important directions in which that work had been taken by Marxist thinkers such as Georg Lukács (1885–1971) and Walter Benjamin (1892–1940). Arendt's work is resistant to any attempt to attribute it to a particular 'school' of critical thought. One aim of the following exploration will be to show how Arendt's work allows us to revisit some of the familiar concerns of later theory, but from a perspective which is unshackled by some of its internal debates and orthodoxies.

THE CATEGORY OF THE WORLD

A key argument of Arendt's work as a whole, mounted most meticulously in *The Human Condition* (1958), is that modern culture has lost touch with a tradition of speech and action that dates back to the classical civilisation of the Greeks and Romans. She thought that the consequences of this loss were nothing short of disastrous.

> To live together in the world means essentially that a world of things is between those who have it in common, as a table is located between those who sit around it; the world, like every in-between, relates and separates men at the same time.

(HC: 52)

This passage gives a good sense of what at first sight can seem peculiar about Arendt's writing. In particular, it gives a taste of its apparently simplistic surface, which almost seems to have the quality of a Christian parable. The ideas beneath this surface are, however, complex and exciting.

Arendt claims that the loss of the political tradition of antiquity entails a loss of the world itself. But what does she mean by 'world'? In comparing the world to a table, Arendt defines it as something which is made, something which is the product of human work. This work involves taking raw material from nature – in the case of a table, wood – and transforming it, refashioning it in order to satisfy human needs. One of the most important of these needs, for Arendt, is community, and the image of the table also suggests that the world is something that, like a table, creates the possibility of community between different people. It does so by relating and separating them at the same time. Sitting around a table creates space and distance between people, it separates them, but at the same time the table fills that space with itself, and allows them to share the space between them. In a similar way, for Arendt, the 'world' created by culture creates the space between different individuals which is needed in order for them to recognise and to acknowledge one another. It does so by filling that space with its works, the 'things' produced in cultural activity, such as works of art.

While Arendt defines community as a condition of human together-ness, the image of the world as a table suggests that distance is also an important factor in Arendt's account of community. While the table, in Arendt's parable, relates men to one another, it also separates them and preserves a distance between them. In strong contrast with this image, Arendt sometimes defines the experience of life in a totalitar-ian state as a condition of 'total domination', which operates by 'destroying all space between men and pressing men against each other' (OT3: 176). One of the major experiences of political modernity, the experience of totalitarian rule, has had the effect of destroying the space between people that is created by the human world.

But this loss of the world neither began nor ended with the downfall of Hitler. In a different way, Arendt also thought that post-war consumer society furthered the destruction of this common world. Arendt thought that a life which is dependent on the consumption of commodities destroys the stable structure of the world, and leaves man in a condition of loneliness. The effect of both totalitarian rule and consumer culture has then been to destroy community and public life.

SOCIETY

While Arendt's image of the common world as a table might seem to have strongly Christian overtones, she is heavily reliant on the ancient Greeks for her understanding of what makes up that world, and in particular for her definition of public space. According to the ancient Greek philosopher Aristotle, a rigid distinction needs to be drawn between home/family life (the *oikos*) and the public life of the city (the *polis*). This distinction will be explored in more detail in the following chapter. The key point for Arendt is that there was a major difference, for the ancient Greeks, in the way that the communal lives of the family and the state were organised. Arendt thought that this distinction between public and private life had become lost in the modern world. In particular, she thought that the ancient distinction between the public and the private had been disrupted by the rise of the distinctively modern phenomenon of 'society'. Arendt writes in *The Human Condition*:

> Society is the form in which the fact of mutual dependence for the sake of life and nothing else assumes public significance and where the activities connected with sheer survival are permitted to appear in public.
>
> (HC: 46)

The rise of modern society, which Arendt dated from the late eighteenth century, has had the effect that the public, political realm has become preoccupied with issues that, in Arendt's terms, are the concern of the private sphere, the sphere of the home and family. Arendt was troubled by the rise of society, but she was also troubled by the rise of modern intellectual disciplines, such as political economy, psychology and sociology, which, under cover of an apparently objective analysis of society, appeared to her to validate and to legitimise modern society. Like others of her generation, then, such as the Frankfurt School critical theorists Theodor Adorno (1903–69) and Max Horkheimer (1895–1973), as well as Heidegger, Arendt sought to develop a type of critical thinking which contests the normalisation and validation of social reality at the hands of the social sciences. To Arendt, modern society did not seem to be a 'natural' and 'obvious' condition of human life; rather, it seemed to be strange, terrifying, even uncanny.

THE FRENCH REVOLUTION

Arendt thought that modern society had emerged in the late 1700s, which was also the period when two major political revolutions took place, first in America (1777) and later in France (1789). One of Arendt's most widely discussed works is her essay *On Revolution* (1963), and she is remembered as an important theorist of revolution. In her essay, Arendt argues that the French Revolution of 1789 was a key event in the conversion of politics into a preoccupation with private welfare that defines modern society. Arendt thought that this revolution made the welfare of the poorest members of society an issue of central public concern.

HUMAN NATURE, ROUSSEAU AND THE FRENCH REVOLUTION

A key intellectual influence on the French Revolution was the social theorist, novelist and philosopher, Jean-Jacques Rousseau (1712–78). Rousseau argued that the human being is naturally good and sympathetic, and feels 'an innate repugnance […] to see his fellow creatures suffer' (OR: 81). Rousseau was profoundly critical of his contemporary society, which he thought had fatally corrupted this natural goodness by making men competitive, self-centred and unmoved by the suffering of the poorest members of society. Rousseau also argued that man is the bearer of natural rights. In the famous first sentence of his political treatise, *The Social Contract* (1762), he wrote that 'Man is born free, and everywhere he is in chains' (Rousseau 1987: 17). The problem that Rousseau sought to resolve in his book was how to find a form of civil association that preserved this natural right to freedom in civil society. The French Revolution's leaders, and in particular Maximilien Robespierre (1758–94), tried to put Rousseau's theory for the state into practice, to release man from his chains, with disastrous consequences. The French Revolution offered Arendt a key example of what happens when political revolution is based on an idealistic view of human nature. In her view, Rousseau's theories translated into Robespierre's 'despotism of liberty against tyranny' (BPF: 139).

Arendt was profoundly troubled by the theory of 'natural rights' that the French revolutionaries tried to put into practice. In contrast to Rousseau, Arendt thought that freedom is something made in the world by human beings acting together, and not something that belongs to every human individual as a natural birthright. The consequences of advocating an idea of natural rights were, Arendt thought, catastrophic in the case of the French Revolution.

CASE STUDY 1: ARENDT AND EDMUND BURKE

In *On Revolution*, Arendt finds a good deal of consonance between her views about society and the famous attack on the principles of the French Revolution launched by the British politician and philosopher Edmund Burke (1729–97) in his *Reflections on the Revolution in France* (1790). For Burke, the mistake of the French experiment in revolutionary government was to make reason rather than custom the basis of government. This rational form of government was enshrined in the Revolution's Declaration of the Rights of Man of 1789 which, following Rousseau, recognised the natural equality and liberty of all men. Burke wrote of the Rights of Man that 'The pretended rights of these theorists are all extremes; and in proportion as they are metaphysically true, they are morally and politically false' (Burke 1999: 443).

Burke draws a key distinction between, on the one hand, theory, metaphysics and truth, and on the other, morality and politics. Arendt also thought that the French Revolution was founded on a false idea of theoretical truth:

> [T]he preparation of the French *hommes de lettres* [men of letters, i.e. thinkers] who were to make the Revolution was theoretical in the extreme […] They had no experiences to fall back upon, only ideas and principles untested by reality to guide and inspire them, and these had all been conceived, formulated and discussed prior to the Revolution.
>
> (OR: 120)

Arendt and Burke both thought that the experiment in a new type of egalitarian society proposed by the French Revolution had relied on 'theory' in place of experience. The danger with theory, for both of them, is that it seeks to make reality fit with its preformed ideas. This attempt by theory to impose a systematic understanding onto the world leads to violence, as the theorists seek to make a diverse and plural reality conform to the unity and singularity of their guiding idea.

THE MEANING OF REVOLUTION

Was Arendt a political reactionary? She undoubtedly presented something of a tragic view of the condition of political modernity. An ancient distinction between public and private spaces has, she argued, become lost with the rise of modern society. But Arendt's critical attitude towards the French Revolution comes from her sense of how the 'theorists' who ran the revolution had taken the power away from the French people to actually change things in their own interests, rather than from any desire to keep things as they are. In the words of her biographer, Arendt's 'plea for conservatism was the vehicle for a revolutionary impulse'. (Young-Bruehl 2004: 317)

Arendt was far from being an anti-revolutionary, let alone a reactionary. In fact, she thought that modern revolutions have never been revolutionary enough. Woven through her telling of the story of the failure of the modern experiment in revolutionary society is a crucial claim mounted by Arendt's work as a whole. If humans could develop their capacity to act spontaneously, freely and in concord, the power of their undertakings would be immeasurable. But modern social experience ill-equips them to fulfil this capacity for authentic and meaningful action. The modern world testifies instead to the dominance of ideas and social theories about what a just society would be like, and what needs to be done to attain it. For Arendt, these theories claim to tell us the meaning of action before acts are even undertaken, and in the process they do violence to the creative possibility of human action. Arendt wanted to imagine a type of revolutionary action that would be unpremeditated, and so would not conform to the expectations of theory. In particular, she wanted revolutionary action to spring forth out of an awareness of tradition, rather than to be dictated to by theoretical ideas of a redeemed future. Like her friend Walter Benjamin, Arendt thought of revolutionary action as 'a tiger's leap into the past' (Benjamin 1992: 253).

CONCLUSION

Arendt's work offers a sustained attempt to tell and retell the story of twentieth-century political history as she had both understood and experienced it. It seeks to warn its readers about the dangers of imposing systematising theories onto the unique form and character of events. It therefore offers a particular, and often provocative, version of those events. The intention is to provoke: to inspire debate in the pursuit of a meaningful account of events, rather than to present the 'truth' of them. Arendt's aim to defend the spontaneity and creative potential of revolutionary action also explains why Arendt advocated stories over theories as a way of understanding events. Stories, unlike theories, do not claim to know the meaning of events before they have even happened. Instead, stories always come after the event. As Arendt wrote in *The Human Condition*, 'Action reveals itself fully only to the storyteller, that is, to the backward glance of the historian' (HC 192).

2

THINKING AND SOCIETY

This chapter will begin to look in detail at one of Arendt's most widely read works, *The Human Condition* (1958). It will outline in detail two aspects of her general argument, firstly her attack on the philosophical tradition, and secondly her critique of modern society. These are key areas of Arendt's thought as a whole, and the reading of *The Human Condition* offered here will aim to open up some of the pathways into her thought that will be followed in this study. It will also provide a first point of contact with Arendt's use of literary examples to elucidate her ideas about politics by examining, in conclusion, her reading of Herman Melville's story *Billy Budd* from *On Revolution* (1963).

The Human Condition is an extraordinary book. It tells the story of how modern man's understanding of himself, his society and his actions continues to be shaped by an inherited philosophical and theological world view, even though modernity understands itself to have initiated a radical break with the past. Reflecting on her life's work in her last, incomplete study, *The Life of the Mind* (1977), Arendt wrote:

> I have clearly joined the ranks of those who for some time now have been attempting to dismantle metaphysics, and philosophy with all its categories, as we have known them from their beginning in Greece until today. Such dismantling is possible only on the assumption that the thread of tradition is broken and that we shall not be able to renew it.
>
> (LM: 212)

For Arendt, as for other, more recent critical thinkers such as the deconstructive philosopher Jacques Derrida (1930–2004), such a 'dismantling of metaphysics' is no simple operation, because inherited philosophical categories continue to determine the way in which we see the world in fundamental ways. In his essay 'Structure, Sign and Play in the Discourse of the Human Sciences', Derrida argued that 'There is no sense in doing without the concepts of metaphysics in order to shake metaphysics. We have no language – no syntax and no lexicon – which is foreign to this history' (Derrida 1978: 280). For both Derrida and Arendt, modernity continues to be conditioned by metaphysics in such a fundamental way that any claim to have stepped outside of the metaphysical tradition needs to be treated with a degree of caution.

THINKING VERSUS ACTING

In *The Human Condition*, Arendt describes this ongoing, unconscious dependence on tradition in terms of the relationship between thinking and acting, which is a key distinction in her thought as a whole. She describes how modern society thinks that it has broken radically with the medieval Christian world view, which understood the monastic life of contemplation and prayer as a 'higher' life than the active, worldly life of work and action. Modernity, for Arendt, is characterised instead by a new faith in the power of human action to change and to improve the world. But the self-understanding of modernity remains, in Arendt's view, shackled by the older theological and philosophical categories that it thinks it has surmounted, and which have traditionally looked down on action. The modern world therefore presents abundant evidence of a paradoxical situation: everywhere, man has come to value industriousness and activity over thought and reflection, but the meaning of his activity and industriousness remains completely hidden from him.

SPACE TRAVEL AND 'WORLD ALIENATION'

An example from the very beginning of Arendt's book should help to clarify what is meant here. In the year before *The Human Condition* was published, 1957, the Soviet Union had launched a satellite into space for the first time. Arendt was fascinated by what the space race, and the attitudes of the two superpowers involved in it, disclosed about the modern world.

> This event, second in importance to no other, not even to the splitting of the atom, would have been greeted with unmitigated joy if it had not been for the uncomfortable military and political circumstances attending it. But, curiously enough, this joy was not triumphal [...] The immediate reaction, expressed on the spur of the moment, was relief about the first 'step toward escape from men's imprisonment to the earth'. And this strange statement, far from being the accidental slip of some American reporter, unwittingly echoed the extraordinary line which, more than twenty years ago, had been carved on the funeral obelisk of one of Russia's great scientists: 'Mankind will not remain bound to the earth forever.'
>
> (HC: 1)

Arendt understands space exploration as a key event in the technological development of modernity. It typifies a crucial aspect of modern culture: its ambition to break free from the limited and bounded condition of life on earth. But Arendt argues that this ambition is not originally a modern one. Instead, she argues that modernity has inherited this ambition to break free from the earth from an older, religious and philosophical world view. The desire to travel through space is, in her view, the modern equivalent of the medieval mystic's longing to escape from the condition of the human flesh into a more godly, spiritual or transcendental realm.

A few pages after describing these responses to the Soviet space probe, Arendt summarises the purpose of the 'historical analysis' proposed by *The Human Condition* as:

> to trace back modern world alienation, its twofold flight from the earth into the universe and from the world into the self, to its origins, in order to arrive at an understanding of the nature of society as it had developed and presented itself at the very moment when it was overcome by the advent of a new and unknown age.
>
> (HC: 6)

In other words, the desire to explore space is, in Arendt's view, a legacy of the ancient philosophical attitude of 'world alienation'.

Modernity remains characterised by this 'world alienation', a desire to escape from the condition of being in the world, even in its most sublime feats of technological production. While the technological development of modernity that allows travel in space is a genuinely new phenomenon, the motivation behind it is, in Arendt's view, philosophically ancient: a desire to escape from the limited, human world into the limitless sphere of the non-human.

THE HUMAN CONDITION, STORYTELLING AND MEANING

Arendt understood the world as a public, shared and politically defined space in which people can debate issues of common interest. She was therefore deeply troubled by the desire to escape from the human conditions of plurality and worldliness, even as she acknowledged it as a fundamental human characteristic. For her, human life is inherently bounded and limited. Moreover the limitations that define the human condition are, according to Arendt, precisely what make that life meaningful. Any life is bounded by two fundamental events: the beginning of life in birth and its ending in death. It is this having a beginning and an ending that confers a unique identity and meaning on a particular life, turning it into what Arendt describes as 'a recognizable life-story from birth to death' (HC: 19).

The fact that the human condition is limited allows that condition to be the subject of story and narrative. However, the story of an individual life cannot be told by the person who lives that life. It is, rather, a story which is ultimately told by others, those who survive the event of that person's death, and can therefore see the whole story. The bounded human condition allows life to be meaningful, yet this meaning is ultimately available to the community that survives the death of the 'hero' of the story. Community, rather than the single individual, is for Arendt the real source of meaning. Arendt claims that, 'Although everybody started his life by inserting himself into the human world through action and speech, nobody is the author or producer of his own life-story' (HC: 184). This also implies that in our search for meaning in our lives we are 'dependent on others, to whom we appear in a distinctness which we ourselves are unable to perceive' (HC: 243).

SOCIETY AND 'INNER EXILE'

Any attempt to escape from the world risks sacrificing the meaning that is tied to the human condition. Clearly, space flight is a particularly dramatic image for this desire to escape from the world; but modernity is also, according to Arendt, defined by a flight 'from the world into the self'. Where space flight takes man away from the world, this flight into the self occurs as a form of inner exile, whereby individual selves reject the common, human world in favour of their own company.

This 'inner' world alienation is a crucial factor in Arendt's account of the collapse of public culture in the nineteenth century, and the subsequent rise of totalitarianism (see Chapters 6 and 7). But Arendt thought that the flight from the world into the self was first tested out in the Romantic art that developed across Europe in the latter half of the eighteenth century.

ROMANTICISM

According to Arendt, during the Romantic period, from the late eighteenth century to the early nineteenth century, modern society first began to take on definition. Society began to erode the freedom of the public, political realm with a new culture of consumerism and conformism. The Romantic art that flourished at this period has often been interpreted as a deliberate reaction against this new commercial society. Romantic writers often turned against the values of this new society in favour of values associated with intimacy and artistic creativity. The English Romantic poet William Wordsworth (1770–1850) wrote in 1802 of how 'the encreasing accumulation of men in cities' was having the effect of reducing their minds 'to a state of almost savage torpor' (Wordsworth and Coleridge 1963: 249). Arendt associated the rejection of society in favour of a new intimacy and self-involvement with the work of Jean-Jacques Rousseau, who was a crucial influence on romanticism. She writes that 'The rebellious reaction against society during which Rousseau and the Romanticists discovered intimacy was directed first of all against the levelling demands of the social, against what we would call today the conformism inherent in every society.' (HC: 39)

'World alienation', the desire to escape from the common, public world, was nothing new according to Arendt. It had its roots in the ancient philosophical and the medieval theological world views, as well as in the Romantic art produced at the beginning of modern society. It was only in the twentieth century, however, that this escape had become possible. Technology had equipped man with the potential physically to leave the earth altogether, by journeying into space – or indeed, in the case of atomic weapons, with the capacity to destroy the world, and with it the human condition of life itself. In a different way, the rise of a society that demands that everyone be alike, that coerces individuals into consumerism and conformism, has so poisoned the public world that individuals are increasingly driven by a need to escape from it altogether into introspection and solitude. It is only, then, in the twentieth century that escape from the world has become a real possibility, rather than a philosopher's dream or an artistic experiment.

'WORLD ALIENATION': THE PHILOSOPHICAL BACKGROUND

Where does this desire for 'world alienation' come from? *The Human Condition* traces the genealogy of world alienation back to the work of the ancient Greek philosopher Plato. Plato is a crucial thinker for Arendt because he was the first to define the public world as a world of illusion and deceptive appearances, and to privilege the other-worldly realm of pure ideas, available only to the philosopher, as the source of true meaning. He did this in his famous allegory of the cave from Book VII of his inquiry into politics, *The Republic*.

PLATO'S ALLEGORY OF THE CAVE

In his allegory, Plato records a dialogue between his teacher, Socrates, and one of Socrates' other pupils, Glaucon, about the relation between the philosopher and the public world. Socrates describes how most men live their lives in a condition of illusion and restriction that only the philosopher, who is preoccupied with higher things, such as the ideas of truth and beauty, can see through. Socrates argues that this alienation from his fellow men and their deluded concerns, para-doxically, means that the philosopher is the best equipped of all men to rule. Socrates asks Glaucon to imagine the human condition as a kind of imprisonment.

> See human beings as though they were in an underground cave-like dwelling with its entrance, a long one, open to the light across the whole width of the cave. They are in it from childhood with their legs and necks in bonds so that they are fixed, seeing only in front of them, unable because of the bonds to turn their heads all the way around. Their light is from a fire burning far above and behind them. Between the fire and the prisoners there is a road above, along which see a wall, built like the partitions puppet-handlers set in front of the human beings and over which they show the puppets.
>
> (Plato 1991: 193)

Because these human beings have always been imprisoned in the cave, they do not know that they are prisoners. For the same reason, they do not know that the shadows that they see cast on the wall by the fire are a reflection, an illusion like a puppet show, rather than real goings-on. There are then three key points to be drawn out of Plato's allegory of the cave for Arendt. One is that, according to Plato, what we see in our lives is fundamentally an illusion – that what we perceive is an effect, a series of shadows cast by a light which we cannot see. Because we cannot see the light, the source of the illusion, and because the shadows constitute all that we have ever seen, we do not know, secondly, that we are perceiving an illusion, nor that there is another, higher and truer world which determines our own. The third key point that Plato makes is that we are coerced into this condition of illusion, and always have been, since we have been chained in the cave since childhood.

The allegory of the cave is, in Arendt's view, a crucial source for many ideas in modern social thought, perhaps most notably for Marxist theories of ideology. The Marxist treatment of ideology suggests that our social relations depend upon an illusion, whereby invisible, ideological forces make us do things, they make us behave in a certain way in society without our knowing that they are determining our behaviour (see Chapter 3). Plato claims that it is only the philosopher who can escape from the cave into the bright light of the realm of ideas. The philosopher is the only one who knows that the illusion is an illusion. Consequently, the philosopher becomes ill at ease and lonely in a society enchained by illusions that he has seen through.

TRUTH VERSUS PERSUASION

This notion of social relations as fundamentally coercive and illusory, and of philosophy as free of illusion, is one that Arendt wanted to challenge. In a lecture that she gave at Notre Dame University in 1954, Arendt described the ways in which Plato's thought set the tone for later philosophical world alienation. It did so by defining an irre-solvable conflict between the typically philosophical form of thinking, or 'dialectic' as it is often called, and 'the specifically political form of speech' (PP: 79) which is persuasion. Plato thought that persuasion, the attempt to persuade others of one's opinion, was not to be trusted, since it is bound up with the illusions of the cave. Arendt argued in her lecture that Plato's suspicion has been very influential on later philosophies, but also later societies than the ancient Greek and how they understand their relation to politics.

For Arendt, Plato's rejection of persuasion in favour of dialectic meant a rejection of the idea that people might hold different opinions that can seem equally valid, and that the world might appear differ-ently to different people, according to their differing standpoints on reality. By turning away from the public realm of speech and persua-sion, Plato put his faith in ideas that are available only to the philo-sopher, who, with his dialectical thinking, has (according to Plato) seen through the illusions of the cave. These ideas are, as such, beyond all speech and persuasion, and all appearance: they exist in a separate realm of absolute truth. Arendt thought that Plato's philosophy fun-damentally rejected the practice of politics, and that it turned away definitively from the public world. But even more worryingly, Plato thought that the public realm should actually be ruled by philosophical ideas. Arendt therefore describes Plato's ideal Republic as an 'ideocracy', a state ruled by ideas (PP: 77).

Arendt sought to turn Plato, and the philosophical tradition that he inspired, right on its head. While public space, the space of appearance, can never give access to 'truth', the realm of abstract ideas, she thought that persuasion enables the formation of a meaningful world view. Arendt argued for the need to accept plurality, the holding of different opinions, as a fundamental human condition. She also thought that it is important to respect 'speech', the rhetorical art of persuasion, as a way of bringing about a reconciliation between these different opinions. Arendt claims in her lecture that 'the world opens up differently to every man, according to his position in it' (PP: 80). Although we appear in public, a realm where things may be different than they seem to us, this does not mean to say that we can, or indeed should, want to abandon the public realm altogether.

PLATO AND THE RISE OF THEORY

Arendt thought that the entire philosophical tradition had been coloured by Plato's distrust for politics and political speech. But this is not to say that philosophy had turned away from politics altogether. Recognising its incongruity with the public realm, philosophy in the form that Plato set it out had developed a tradition of political theory that sought to dominate that realm, and to organise it in the interests of philosophical knowledge and the philosophical way of life. Arendt agued that this tradition of political theory was inherited from the Greeks by Christian culture:

> [T]he enormous superiority of contemplation over activity of any kind, action not excluded, is not Christian in origin. We find it in Plato's political philosophy, where the whole utopian reorganization of *polis* life is not only directed by the superior insight of the philosopher but has no aim other than to make possible the philosopher's way of life. Aristotle's very articulation of the different ways of life, in whose order the life of pleasure plays a minor role, is clearly guided by the ideal of contemplation (*theōria*).
>
> (HC: 14)

By arguing that the philosopher's way of life is the ideal way of life, philosophy, in Arendt's view, had done violence to the reality of other forms of human activity by always comparing them unfavourably with the philosophical life committed to 'theory' or contemplation. The kinds of activity that have seemed inferior to thinking for philosophers and theologians through the ages include political speech, but also activities that induce pleasure, such as the appreciation of art. In the above passage, Arendt traces the inheritance of this attitude into Christian culture, which translated Aristotle's understanding of the life of thought, or *theōria*, into the monastic notion of contemplation. Arendt thought that Christianity's hostility to the human body was also taken from Plato and Aristotle. For Plato, according to Arendt, the body is synonymous with politics and the political realm, and the soul is synonymous with philosophy. Therefore, the more a philosopher becomes a true philosopher, 'the more he will separate himself from his body' (PP: 93).

Arendt thought that this dismissive attitude towards the reality and complexity of human action survives even into the work of key modern philosophers who claimed to have escaped the lofty pose of ancient theory. Focusing in particular on Karl Marx and Friedrich Nietzsche, Arendt argued that even when modern philosophers sought to challenge the dominance of *theōria*, by developing alternative ideas of 'life' (in the case of Nietzsche) and labour (in the case of Marx), they remained, albeit without realising it, bound to this privileging of thought. There is a curious paradox, then, in that Karl Marx is famous as a thinker of praxis and material social relations, but that his treatment of production, according to Arendt, remained entirely within the anti-political philosophical tradition.

MARX

The reason why modern philosophers such as Marx are, in Arendt's view, basically Platonic in outlook, and therefore incapable of thinking about what politics really means, is because they are theorists of society rather than of politics. The political and the social are, for Arendt, very distinct but overlapping notions. Marx was not truly 'political' in Arendt's terms because his concern was essentially with social welfare and economics rather than with political speech and action. Arendt thought that Marx, like Plato before him, had understood the political realm to be governed by illusion.

> In the modern world, the social and the political realms are much less distinct [than in the ancient]. That politics is nothing but a function of society, that action, speech and thought are primarily superstructures upon social interest, is not a discovery of Karl Marx but on the contrary is among the axiomatic assumptions Marx accepted uncritically from the political economists of the modern age.
>
> (HC: 33)

For Arendt, what is distinctive about modern society as a way of life is that private interests have become a matter of public concern, and an ancient distinction between public and private realms has been blurred.

Crucially, the development of modern society has meant that the unique purpose of public space, to guarantee a free exchange of ideas in the form of speech, has been lost altogether. This distinction between public space and private space is key to Arendt's thought as a whole, and we need to pause and look at it in more detail.

PUBLIC VERSUS PRIVATE

According to Aristotle in his *Politics*, the life of the citizen is to be divided up between two rigidly separate spheres, the home (*oikos*) and the city (*polis*). The rules that governed the home were considered by Aristotle to be separate and different from the rules governing the city. This was because '[t]he distinctive trait of the household sphere was that in it men lived together because they were driven by their wants and needs' (HC: 30). The ancient family or household, according to Arendt in her reading of Aristotle, served to satisfy natural, bodily needs, the needs of the physical, material human self for shelter, food and comfort. Since the bodily conditions of appetite and need are involuntary, since they are not things that could be chosen at will or opted out of, the *oikos* was, for the ancient Greeks, a space ruled by necessity. In other words, because we are tied to our appetites and our bodies in the *oikos*, we can never be free there. The body, according to Aristotle's way of imagining human life, is therefore the ultimate human condition: that which binds us to the earth and restricts the reach of our freedom. The *polis*, by contrast, was 'the sphere of freedom', and the condition of entering into the freedom of the *polis* came from 'mastering the necessities of life' (HC: 30). For the ancient Athenians, this mastery over necessity came through the ownership of slaves, who carried out the labour necessary to the life of the *oikos*.

Ancient politics, the business of the *polis*, was conducted through speech, understood as the free articulation of opinions and the attempt to persuade others. The domestic sphere of the *oikos*, on the other hand, was governed by violence. Arendt claims that 'force and violence are justified in this sphere because they are the only means to master necessity' (HC: 31). The law of the *oikos* could never appear in public because 'violence itself is incapable of speech' (OR 19). Speech, in other words, is taken by Arendt to be the mark of politics and civilisation. The critical thinker Slavoj Žižek (1949–) writes that 'entry into language and the renunciation of violence are often understood as two aspects of one and the same gesture' (Žižek 2008: 52). This opposition between speech and violence, and the idea of civilisation as a realm of free speech that this opposition underpins, has been attacked by a number of critical thinkers, including the psychoanalyst Jacques Lacan (1901–81) and the deconstructive philosopher Jacques Derrida, who have wanted to describe speech as involved with acts of violence. However, Arendt holds fast to the need for this distinction.

According to Arendt, the consequences of the blurring of the distinction between public and private spheres in modern society have been catastrophic. The importing of what should be strictly private concerns into the public sphere contaminates public space with the violence that, for the Greeks, characterised the private realm. What gets lost in society is the diversity of freely held opinions. According to Arendt, 'society always demands that its members act as though they were members of one enormous family which has only one opinion and one interest' (HC: 39).

SOCIETY AND ACTION

Much of Arendt's work is characterised by an account of the effects of socialisation on the modern self, as well as a fierce rebuttal of the kinds of modern, pseudo-scientific social theory which seemed to her to validate and legitimise the distorted experiences of that self. *The Origins of Totalitarianism*, in particular, offers an alternative sociology of the late nineteenth century and early twentieth century, that looks at the consequences for the human personality of membership of types of mass society that, for Arendt, took away the freedom of that individual personality and replaced it with a crushing conformism. Arendt also touches on this point in *The Human Condition*, where the social-scientific notion of 'behaviourism' provokes her particular ire:

> It is decisive that society, on all its levels, excludes the possibility of action, which formerly was excluded from the household. Instead, society expects from each of its members a certain kind of behaviour, imposing innumerable and various rules, all of which tend to 'normalize' its members, to make them behave, to exclude spontaneous action or outstanding achievement.
>
> (HC: 40)

The idea of 'behaviour' implies acting according to a particular code or rule which conscribes individual action – in other words, conforming to social expectation. More recently, this notion of behaviour has been described as 'peer pressure', the imposition of norms of action onto the individual, which must be fulfilled in order that he or she gain social acceptance. Modern society, then, is intrinsically bound up with unfreedom and violent coercion for Arendt. It takes away the creative, spontaneous potential of human action, replacing it with the demand that separate individuals behave in the same way. In a later essay, *On Violence* (1970), Arendt claims that it is 'the function [...] of all action, as distinguished from mere behaviour, to interrupt what otherwise would have proceeded automatically and therefore predictably' (CR: 132–33). As things stand, however, Arendt thought that forms of societal control over human action take away the very possibility that we might act in a way that isn't premeditated, or that doesn't follow a script.

CONCLUSIONS

Arendt's argument in *The Human Condition* tells a story of the genealogy of modernity that takes an exceptionally long view. Its assumption is that we need first to understand the ancient Greek experience of philosophy, and the ancient Greek division between domestic and political life, in order to make sense of the divisive and conformist social experience of modernity. This long view also helps to explain why, for Arendt, supposedly radical critiques of the modern social condition, such as Marxism, turn out to be part of the problem. Arendt's work then proposes an exhilarating departure from this whole tradition in favour of an enquiry into what the real possibilities of human action might be, if action could be liberated from the divisiveness both of social experience and of philosophical tradition. We will look in more detail at this enquiry in the next chapter.

Such a radical departure from the whole of Western thought and social experience had, by definition, no inherited methodology by which to support itself and to define its inquiry. For Arendt, storytelling became a key point of departure for this exhilarating new way of thinking. *The Human Condition* is itself a kind of story, the story of how modernity receives its identity from a tradition that it thinks it has surmounted. But Arendt was also an exceptionally acute and original reader of the stories told by others. She understood modern writing, particularly since the Romantic period, as a crucial record of the problems with social experience that her work also seeks to address. To conclude this chapter, we will examine Arendt's reading of Herman Melville's story *Billy Budd* (1924), in order to illustrate in a more concrete way her core ideas about the loss of politics in modern social experience.

CASE STUDY 2: BILLY BUDD

One of the more unpalatable aspects of Arendt's argument for the contemporary reader is its wilful abandonment of any attachment to nature or the 'natural' world as a sphere of intrinsic value. For Arendt, nature was essentially associated with a lack of freedom, with necessity and, ultimately, with violence. 'Nature', in this view, is the domain of the private, the realm of the body and of family relationships. It is the sphere from which the individual must liberate himself in order to become a fully public citizen, and a member of the *polis*. Arendt's claim is that nature must remain firmly within the private realm. One way of understanding mass society, for Arendt, is as an 'unnatural growth […] of the natural' (HC: 47). In other words, she thinks of totalitarian states as spaces in which natural forces have overgrown and suffocated the public sphere. For an age like our own, in which environmental concerns are, justifiably, a central public preoccupation, this can seem like a very unpleasant claim. It also conflicts with a typically post-Romantic view of nature as, in the words of one Arendt critic, 'a stable, comforting setting for human life, far less hostile than the artificial world of modern cities' (Canovan 1992: 107), and with Rousseau's notion that man is the bearer of natural rights (see Chapter 1).

In her essay *On Revolution* (1963), Arendt reads Herman Melville's story, *Billy Budd*, as an allegory of the failure of the politics of the French Revolution. She thought that, in his story, Melville 'knew how to talk back directly to the men of the French Revolution and to their proposition that man is good in a state of nature and becomes wicked in society' (OR: 83). Her reading of Melville is also a useful example of how Arendt uses storytelling as a way of combating the violence that theory does to human experience.

Melville's story is set in the French revolutionary wars, and concerns an English sailor, Billy Budd. Billy has been taken from a merchant vessel which is significantly called the *Rights of Man*, and press-ganged onto a warship, the *Bellipotent*, where he attracts the envy of the ship's Master at Arms, Claggart. Billy Budd, according to Arendt, is a figure of '[g]oodness beyond virtue' and 'natural goodness' (OR: 83); in the story he is perpetually described as a kind of messiah figure and an 'angel of God' (Melville: 51). Billy is, in essence, unworldly, almost messianic, a figure for the natural man of the social theory of the French Revolution. Claggart, on the other hand, is a figure of pure evil, 'evil beyond vice' (OR: 83). In his envy of Billy, Claggart bears him false witness, accusing Billy of fomenting mutiny on the ship, at which Billy, the figure of pure, natural innocence, strikes Claggart dead with a single blow. Arendt writes that the 'greatness of this part of the story lies in that goodness, because it is part of "nature", does not act but merely asserts itself forcefully and, indeed, violently' (OR: 83). The story shows, according to Arendt, how 'natural goodness' is equally capable of violence as pure evil – thus refuting the French revolutionaries' belief in man's natural innocence.

According to Arendt, Billy's story shows that natural goodness cannot 'act' in a public way, but is rather immediately reduced to violence when it appears in public space and is called on to avenge injustice. In the same way, the making public of a concern for the suffering of the poor in the rhetoric of the French revolutionaries led directly, according to Arendt, to violence on the streets of Paris and the guillotining of those who were seen as enemies of the people. Billy strikes Claggart because he cannot defend himself through speech when Claggart bears him false witness; Billy has a stammer and, in the heat of the moment, he cannot speak out against the false accusation. Instead, he resorts to an act of silent violence. He then figures, for Arendt, the tragic and violent consequences that have followed, in modernity, the public appearance of voiceless innocence. This innocence cannot take up a position in the world and negotiate or persuade others; in its own way, therefore, it is tyrannical and absolutist. Arendt writes that 'The absolute – and to Melville an absolute was incorporated in the Rights of Man – spells doom to everyone when it is introduced into the political realm' (OR: 84). Melville's is a story that warns against, and in its particularity offers an alternative to, the absolutism of theory.

3

ACTING

The title of this chapter refers most broadly to the understanding of man as a being who 'acts', or who does things in society, as opposed to an understanding of man as a being who is defined fundamentally by his capacity for thought and reasoning. Arendt thought that, in the modern world, man had come to be defined as an acting rather than a thinking being, and that this definition of him formed a key aspect of the modern world's break with tradition. This chapter will seek to understand why, according to Arendt, man's action has become fundamentally meaningless in modern society. Unlike many of her contemporaries, who we will compare her with in this chapter, Arendt did not think that acting in society was *inherently* meaningless, or that it was impossible for social actors to act in a meaningful way. She took political revolution to be a key example of how action can, under the right conditions, become meaningful in society (see Chapter 1). For Arendt, the question of the meaning of action is tied to the question of what makes a meaningful politics. Arendt's effort to recover a sense of what meaningful social action might be like also led her to consider a more specific type of 'acting' – that is, acting on the stage, in the theatre. The theatre has been used throughout history by philosophers as a metaphor for the fundamental meaninglessness and futility of human action. In this chapter we will look at how Arendt sought to turn the philosophical understanding of the theatre inside out, and to use the example of the theatre as a guide in her effort to understand what meaningful action might be like.

ACTION AND PHILOSOPHY

What does Arendt mean by action? In *The Human Condition*, Arendt describes the ways in which meaningful action can unlock the relation between self and other in society. Action, for Arendt, makes the human self appear in a distinctness that enables the other to recognise who that self really is. Another key argument that Arendt makes about action is that, through art and storytelling, a community can recognise, understand and fundamentally know the meaning of the actions undertaken by members of that community. From the perspective of later critical thinking, these claims might seem idealistic, not to say naive. For critical thinkers working with the Marxist concept of ideology in particular, the meaning of human action remains hidden from the actor, or rather from the ideological subject, who is understood to act in a condition of ideological illusion.

For Arendt, the idea that we act in a condition of illusion is traceable back to Plato, and to the condition of philosophical world alienation that he inaugurated (see Chapter 2). In *The Human Condition*, she wrote the following:

> It is for this reason that Plato thought that human affairs […], the outcome of action (*praxis*) should not be treated with great seriousness; the actions of men appear like the gestures of puppets led by an invisible hand behind the scene, so that man seems to be a kind of a plaything of a god.
>
> (HC: 185)

For Plato, it is axiomatic that man does not know the meaning of his actions. Plato claims that man does not act in freedom, but rather he is a kind of puppet whose strings are pulled by a higher agency that plays with him and of which he is unaware. Recognising this illusion, the Platonic philosopher, like the god that plays with man, refuses to treat his actions with seriousness.

Philosophy seems by this definition to dismiss the possibility that there might be meaning in the acts or the actors themselves, preferring instead to attribute that meaning to impersonal forces which stand behind the scenes and control those acts. For Arendt, this

Platonic view of human action has become a norm for the modern world. For example, the Marxist philosophy of history restricts man's awareness of the meaning of his actions in a similar way. The factory owner who exploits his workers may think that he is simply trying to keep his factory running at a low cost or, if he searches his conscience, he may admit to himself that he is acting from selfish motives. In fact, according to the Marxist analysis, neither of these interpretations explains the real meaning of his actions. According to the Marxist analysis, in exploiting his workers, the factory owner is, in fact, forwarding the interests of his social class, the bourgeoisie, and this is so whether or not he understands himself to belong to that class. The real meaning of his actions is hidden from him by a system of beliefs that he holds about himself, and that misrepresent to him the real social and economic conditions of which he is a part.

For Arendt, this argument about ideology means that Marx, like Plato before him, assumes that only the philosopher can see through the illusions of social life. In a famous passage from his satire on a French *coup d'état* of 1851, *The Eighteenth Brumaire of Louis Bonaparte* (1852), Marx even invokes the same metaphor of the theatre as Plato to describe human political affairs as a condition of deception and illusion.

> Hegel remarks somewhere that all facts and personages of great importance in world history occur, as it were, twice. He forgot to add: the first time as tragedy, the second as farce […] The tradition of all the dead generations lays like a nightmare on the brain of the living. And just when they seem engaged in revolutionizing themselves and things, in creating something that has never yet existed, precisely in such periods of revolutionary crisis they anxiously conjure up the spirits of the past to their service and borrow from them names, battle cries and costumes in order to present the new scene of world history in this time-honoured disguise and this borrowed language.
>
> (Marx 1963: 15)

This passage shows the extent of Marx's disillusionment with a revolutionary uprising that had taken place in 1848, and which had ended, like the revolution of 1789, by reverting to dictatorship just three years later. Just as the living, in 1848, had seemed to be on the cusp of liberating themselves from dead tradition in revolutionary action, just as they seemed to be on the point of 'creating something that never existed', they dressed themselves up in the costume of the dead and played out their mistakes. The tragedy of the French Revolution of 1789 was repeated in 1848 as farce.

CIVIL DISOBEDIENCE

Writing in 1954, Arendt was certainly much more optimistic than Marx in 1852 about the possibility of revolutionary action really changing the order of things. Arendt claimed in a lecture from that year that 'Under present circumstances, true action, namely, the beginning of something new, seems possible only in revolutions' (EU: 437). Later, in an essay written in 1970 called 'Civil Disobedience', she wrote of how '[d]isobedience to the law, civil and criminal' had become 'a mass phenomenon in recent years':

> Viewed from the outside and considered in historical perspective, no clearer writing on the wall – no more explicit sign of the inner instability and vulnerability of existing governments and legal systems – could be imagined.

> (CR: 69)

Arendt's engagement with civil disobedience is both ominous and optimistic. There had been a massive growth in civil disobedience over the course of the 1960s in America and Europe. The immediate causes for this new culture of unrest included racial discrimination, the women's liberation movement and the Vietnam War, as well as a growing culture of student protest, but for Arendt at the root of it was a loss of governmental authority. For Arendt, the civil disobedience and criminal activity practised by people who no longer trusted those in power (and, perhaps even more importantly, the lies and criminal activity of those in power themselves) could well augur the end for 'existing governments'. She had already seen something similar happen in Germany in the 1930s, and Arendt never took for granted the stability and permanence of existing political institutions. Although she was often very cynical about the political activism of the 1960s, a sense that the political situation was not stable, that things might change at any moment, remained an abiding conviction in her later work.

POWER

This openness to the possibility of change was conspicuously absent from the work of many European critical thinkers writing in the wake of the activism of the 1960s. Writing around the same time as Arendt's essay on civil disobedience, the structuralist Marxist philosopher Louis Althusser (1918–90) famously claimed that 'man is an ideological animal by nature' (Althusser 2001: 116). For Althusser, there is no concrete individual who exists 'before' or 'outside' ideological systems of belief; so extensive is the reach of ideology that individual subjects can never step outside of it and therefore, perhaps, never act in freedom. This pessimism is not restricted to Althusser. In an interview given in the late 1970s, the radical social historian Michel Foucault (1926–84) gave the following rather pessimistic assessment of his concept of 'power'.

> If power were never anything but repressive, if it never did anything but to say no, do you really think one would be brought to obey it? What makes power hold good, what makes it accepted, is simply the fact that it doesn't weigh on us as a force that says no, but that it traverses and produces things, it induces pleasure, forms knowledge, produces discourse. It needs to be considered as a productive network that runs through the whole social body, much more than as a negative instance whose function is repression.
>
> (Foucault 1980: 119)

Although Foucault argues that power is not just repressive, that it circulates between different individuals rather than being imposed upon them from above, this circulation of power makes those individuals all the more likely to 'obey' it. For Foucault, power is not something that individuals or social groups can resist easily, since it does more than simply repress them, to prohibit them from doing things. It is also creative and affirmative, enabling them to act in ways that make it very difficult to imagine what acting in a way that is not predetermined by power might mean. Power is clever.

Arendt's work was also preoccupied with questions about power, and she was also interested in the ways in which power organises relationships between individuals. Foucault and Arendt both also conceived of power as connected to ideas of display and appearance. But unlike Foucault, Arendt thought of power as a fundamentally enabling, rather than coercive factor in human social interaction. Power, for Arendt, is something that flows between people when they have freely chosen to be together. It appears when different individuals are together in a public space, and is made manifest through their speech. 'Power', Arendt writes, 'is actualized only where word and deed have not parted company, where words are not empty and deeds not brutal, where words are not used to veil intentions but to disclose realities' (HC: 200). She also thought of power as a 'potential and not an unchangeable, measurable, and reliable entity like force or strength' (HC: 200). Power for Arendt is inherent in human communities, but it is only actualised when people come to act out of a common interest, for example in revolutionary action.

However, Arendt did not find much evidence of power working in contemporary society. The modern social condition, instead, had taken all power away from individuals and invested it in the idea of society itself. Much of the civil disobedience of the 1960s was, in Arendt's view, an expression of violence rather than power. Arendt thought that the abuse of social power was becoming increasingly true for American society, and that it had long been true of European society.

Much of the critical thought that we have compared to Arendt so far in this chapter attributes the meaning of human action to trans-personal, elusive forces that ultimately deceive the actor, such as the gods (in Plato) or class interest (in the case of Marx) or power (in the case of Foucault). Arendt actually thought that critical thinking and philosophy were themselves partly responsible for taking the meaning of their actions away from human beings, by understanding that meaning as essentially an idea. By contrast, Arendt thought that the meaning of action can be made available to the community of which the individual actor is a part through the agency of storytelling.

PROMISES AND FORGIVENESS

Promises and forgiveness are, for Arendt, important forms of inter-action which guarantee that power will abide between individuals in their coming together. They also show that action takes on meaning and definition only in a community. Promising and forgiving others, thought Arendt, released the individual from the condition of solitude and loneliness into which he had been cast by modern social existence.

> Without being forgiven, released from the consequences of what we have
> done, our capacity to act would, as it were, be confined to one single deed
> from which we could never recover; we would remain the victims of its con-
> sequences forever [...] Without being bound to the fulfilment of promises, we
> would never be able to keep our identities; we would be condemned to
> wander helplessly and without direction in the darkness of each man's
> lonely heart.
>
> (HC: 237)

Arendt understood promises existentially, as experiences that can
happen in particular individuals' lives, and that give those lives shape
and meaning. Undertaking to keep promises to others gives, according
to Arendt, continuity to human relationships. It guarantees their
existence into the future. Similarly, forgiveness allows the consequences
of past actions to be undone; it creates the possibility of a new future
by acting as a corrective for 'the inevitable damages resulting from
action' (HC: 239). Real action, for Arendt, always has unpredictable
outcomes. Action might always bring about violence to the human
community, in ways that cannot necessarily be anticipated. This is the
cost of freedom of action. In the light of this, Arendt thought that
promises and forgiveness give some guarantee of worldliness and stability to human actions.

EXISTENTIALISM

Arendt's argument about action in *The Human Condition* resonates in
important ways with other contemporary trends in social and political
thought. Existentialism, and in particular the work of the French
existentialist Jean-Paul Sartre (1905–80), sought to break with traditional philosophy in favour of revolutionary action. As with Arendt,
this proposed break with philosophical tradition was in part brought
about in response to the experience of totalitarian rule and the
Second World War, and was also influenced by the philosophy of
Martin Heidegger. In an early essay, 'French Existentialism' (1946),
Arendt gave the following, rather breathless account of existentialism's
influence on the social life of Paris.

> A lecture on philosophy provokes a riot, with hundreds crowding in and thou-
> sands turned away. Books on philosophical problems preaching no cheap

creed and offering no panacea but, on the contrary, so difficult as to require actual thinking sell like detective stories. Plays in which the action is a matter of words, not of plot, and which offer a dialogue of reflections and ideas run for months and are attended by enthusiastic crowds. [...] Philosophers become newspapermen, playwrights, novelists. They are not members of university faculties but 'bohemians' who stay at hotels and live in the café – leading a public life to the point of renouncing privacy.

(EU: 188)

Arendt was excited by existentialism because it seemed to turn philosophising into a public, revolutionary activity. It took philosophy out of the university onto the streets, and in the process it broke down the distinctions between thought and deed, and between philosophy and literature. Existentialist philosophical treatises, writes Arendt, 'sell like detective stories', while existentialist novels and plays, such as *Huis Clos* by Sartre, deal with intense philosophical problems.

This last claim seems to suggest that, in Arendt's view, existentialism had brought about a reconciliation between drama and philosophy. Where theatre, for philosophers from Plato to Marx, has often been used to symbolise the ways in which man acts in a condition of illusion, whereby he cannot understand the larger forces which are determining his actions 'off scene', for the existentialist, theatre becomes a revolutionary tool that can be used to turn that illusion back on itself. In his plays, Sartre dramatised the absurdity of a bourgeois social condition in which man is forced to act in particular ways, and in which there can be no discernible meaning to his actions. He used drama to expose the ways in which the self is always playing a role in society. According to Arendt, the actor had become an 'ideal' for existentialists because he 'constantly changes his role, and thus can never take any of his roles seriously' (EU: 191). Since he is always playing a role anyway, the actor liberates others from an absurd bourgeois morality that tells them that they must be consistent in their social relations. Arendt thought that this rejection of the very possibility of authentic action in contemporary society meant that existentialism had brought about 'a genuine rebellion of the intellectuals, whose docility in relation to modern society was one of the saddest aspects of the sad spectacle of Europe between the wars' (EU: 188–89).

EXISTENTIALISM AND THE PHILOSOPHICAL TRADITION

When Arendt visited Europe after the Second World War, she became suspicious of the direction taken by the work of the existentialists, and in particular of Sartre. In a lecture given in 1954 entitled 'Concern with Politics in Recent European Philosophical Thought', Arendt summarised the ambitions of existentialism in terms that initially seem very similar to her own. In particular, it proposed 'salvation from thought through action' (EU: 438). Yet Arendt thought that existentialism, despite its claim to be a philosophy of action, offered an incomplete break with the philosophical tradition. This failure to break free from the realm of ideas meant that existentialism, in Arendt's terms, failed to think in a meaningful way about politics – even though existentialists like Sartre spoke out publicly about contemporary political events in France, such as the atrocities committed by the French army and police in the course of the Algerian War of Independence (1954–62). In the same lecture, Arendt claimed that while existentialists put politics 'at the very center of their work', they 'look, on the contrary, to politics for the solution of philosophic perplexities that in their opinion resist solution or even adequate formulation in purely philosophic terms' (EU: 437). Existentialism, according to Arendt, made politics the handmaid of philosophy, and to this extent it remained, in Arendt's view, firmly in line with the Platonic tradition (see Chapter 2). In other words, Arendt thought that politics, for Sartre, had remained a space in which philosophical and theoretical dilemmas are tested out and resolved, rather than a sphere of inherent value.

SOCIOLOGY

Arendt's ideas about action can also be usefully compared to, and contrasted with, the treatment of action in the discipline of sociology. In the English- and German-speaking worlds, sociology has sought, in various ways, to analyse the phenomenon of action in society from a systematic and theoretical, as well as a non-philosophical perspective. The key founding figure for sociology in Germany was Max Weber (1864–1920) who wrote sociological studies of religion and modern bureaucracy. Arendt criticised existentialism for offering an incomplete departure from the philosophical tradition, and therefore for continuing to remain 'theoretical' in its approach to the question of political action. Her critique of sociology, which extends right across her work, works the opposite way around, to the extent that she thought that sociology had broken with philosophical thought in a premature and naive way.

KARL MANNHEIM

In a review that she wrote in 1930 of a key sociological study of the early twentieth century, Karl Mannheim's *Ideology and Utopia* (1929), Arendt contrasts sociology with philosophy in terms of its failure to take any standpoint on social reality. In her review, Arendt compares Mannheim's ideas with those of the critical theorist and Marxist philosopher Georg Lukács. The work of both thinkers, Arendt writes, 'challenges the intellectual sphere's claim to absolute validity' (EU: 29). Both thinkers, in other words, attack a view of social reality that is organised according to philosophical ideas. As a Marxist, Lukács organises his attack on philosophy 'from a specific position, namely, that of the proletariat, and thereby imperceptibly and without any qualms adopts its altogether justified concept of interest' (EU: 29). Mannheim's sociology, by contrast, offers no such critical standpoint on society. It pretends instead to be a scientific, neutral and objective study of social reality. Arendt's point is that the sociologist's claim to offer a neutral, dispassionate understanding of society is self-deluded. In reality, sociology's account of society is anything but neutral and dispassionate. Instead, sociology, by claiming to be a scientific analysis of the condition of social reality, actually inadvertently justifies the socio-economic norms of that reality. It rules out of court the possibility that social life might be something different than it is.

TALCOTT PARSONS

This lack of a critical viewpoint on society is evident in the work of both American and German sociologists. American sociology took a very different and altogether less optimistic view of the concept of power than Arendt. A very popular book among American sociologists at the time that Arendt was writing *The Human Condition* was *The Structure of Social Action* (1937) by Talcott Parsons (1902–79). The critical theorist Jürgen Habermas (1929–) has contrasted Parsons' treatment of action with Arendt's in a very revealing way. According to Habermas, Parsons emphasises how there is power inherent in social systems and structures. For Parsons, power is 'the general capacity to get things done in the interests of collective goals' (Habermas 1977: 5). In making his argument, Parsons shows, according to Habermas, that in order for power to flow through the social system, some element of coercion, some element of 'structural violence' (Habermas 1977: 21) is necessarily inflicted onto the wills of particular individuals. In order to get things done, argues Parsons, the social structure needs to simplify the needs and interests of those individuals in line with the needs and interests of the social group as a whole.

For both Mannheim and Parsons, sociology appears to lack a view of power which understands its potential to liberate individuals from a coercive social space, which is how Arendt chooses to understand power. Parsons understands power to operate by coercing individuals in order to achieve the aims of the social structure as a whole.

SOCIOLOGY AGAINST PHILOSOPHY

If existential thought understands social reality as a condition of inauthentic being against which man must take violent, revolutionary action, sociology, on the contrary, validates and legitimises that social reality. Even worse, sociology fails to think about the consequences of its specific rejection of philosophy and philosophical ideas. Sociology, according to Arendt in her essay on Mannheim, thinks that philosophical thought 'is by nature not at home in the world' (EU: 37). In assuming that thought – not just the inherited philosophical tradition, but the condition of thinking as such – is fundamentally defined by world alienation, sociology rules out the possibility that thinking could ever be anything else. In particular, it rules out the possibility that thinking might find a way to take up a position in the world, rather than remaining alienated from the world. The attempt to give thought a position in the world, to overcome world alienation, is a major ambition of Arendt's work.

Arendt thought that sociology's wholesale rejection of thinking had profound consequences for sociology itself. As long as sociology misconstrues philosophical thinking, by assuming that thought is not at home in the world, it will also misconstrue the social world itself, by assuming that there is no place for thinking in it. Sociology is 'not concerned with reality as such,' writes Arendt in her review of Mannheim, 'but with *reality that exerts power over thought*' (EU: 36). In other words, in trying to give an account of this reality that is more powerful than thought, sociology distorts our perception of 'reality as such'. Reality becomes, in the sociological account of it, something that can overpower thinking.

This very difficult point is actually a crucial one for an understanding of the ambition of Arendt's thought as a whole, as well as her usefulness for students of literature. Arendt is claiming, in effect, that as long as thought remains alienated from the world, not only will the activity of thinking be impoverished, but it will also remain difficult to come up with an adequate critical understanding of social reality. Arendt argues that sociology not only distorts our perception of ideas, it also distorts the perception of the social reality that it wants to detach them from. What is needed, instead, is a reconciliation of thinking to the world that respects the real identity of each. Arendt thought that it was the task of art to bring about a reconciliation of thinking and social reality, in the interests of both.

CASE STUDY 3: ROMANTICISM, IDEOLOGY AND WORLD ALIENATION

It might be worthwhile to pause and step back from Arendt's work here, in order to think through some of the wider implications of her treatment of action. How can literature form a bridge between thinking and reality, world and idea?

Romanticism has long been considered to be a type of art that is closely allied to philosophy. The poetry of leading Romantics such as William Wordsworth in England and Friedrich Hölderlin (1770–1843) in Germany has been read by critical thinkers such as Paul de Man (1919–83) and Martin Heidegger as offering a type of philosophical argument in the form of verse. But in recent years, literary critics working on English romanticism have sought to challenge this association of romanticism and philosophy, and to claim that such an association gives a 'world alienating' view of Romantic poetry.

There is certainly lots of evidence for this attitude of world alienation in Romantic poetry. Wordsworth argued in his autobiographical poem *The Prelude* (1805) that the task of poets is to teach mankind how

the mind of man becomes
A thousand times more beautiful than the earth
On which he dwells.

(Wordsworth 1970: 241)

It is as if the vocation of poets, as Wordsworth understands it, is to make man recognise himself as a being who is no longer associated with the world or the earth, an intellectual being who is self-sufficient, and a being whose mind exceeds and is better, more beautiful than the worldly condition in which it dwells. For literary critics such as Jerome McGann (1937–) in his book *The Romantic Ideology* (1983), such highly Platonic claims in Wordsworth's verse mean that he 'lost the world merely to gain his own immortal soul' (McGann 1983: 88). Wordsworth becomes, as in the title of McGann's book, the chief exponent of a 'Romantic ideology' that wraps itself up in ideas and forgets about the realities of the social world.

In contrast to Wordsworth, McGann suggests ways in which Romantic literature, and literature in general, need not be seen as quite so 'world alienating'. McGann writes in his book *Social Values and Poetic Acts* that:

While imaginative work is more coherent than the world, it is no less exigent and performative *in* the world. Literature is not simply a symbolic or aesthetic structure, it also – and simultaneously – functions as a structure of [social] signification.

(McGann 1987: 7)

The assumption here is that, in order for literature to be understood as 'performative in the world', it must lose its distinctively literary (aesthetic and symbolic) qualities. It is almost as if, for McGann, a work of literature cannot be in the world and remain a work of art. Or at least, the way in which it remains a work of art in the world is by being 'performative', or by playing a role.

Where might Arendt stand on all of this? We might expect her to share in the critical attitude towards philosophical world alienation that is found in McGann's work. In fact she, like many others of her generation including the critical theorist Theodor Adorno and Heidegger (see Chapter 4), was highly suspicious of any attempt to reduce art to the status of social ideology. For Arendt, art served a crucial role in reconciling thinking to the world.

THEATRE AND ACTION

Arendt thought that the contribution to the world offered by art, and in particular by storytelling, was to provide an understanding of the unique and differing identities of human beings. Whenever philosophy has tried to define man, it has always done so by thinking about him in the abstract, as a particular type of 'thinking' being, rather than by thinking about how meaning is disclosed in particular men's actions. Not only this, but, according to Arendt, philosophy has always been preoccupied by the notion that there is a higher power behind man pulling the strings and giving his life meaning. In Arendt's view, the question: What is man? has therefore always been translated, from the philosophical point of view, into another question: What is man for? What is his purpose or vocation in the world? Philosophy has always taken a very instrumental view of man: it has assumed that he has been created for a specific purpose, and that it is the job of philosophy to find out what that purpose is.

Art, by contrast, does not pose this question of what man's purpose might be. Rather, it is a space in which the question: What is man? can be posed by looking at the particular life-stories of individual men. As Arendt writes in *The Human Condition*:

> The real story in which we are engaged as long as we live has no visible or invisible maker because it is not made. The only "somebody" it reveals is its hero, and it is the only medium in which the originally intangible manifestation of a uniquely distinct "who" can become tangible […] through action and speech. *Who* somebody is or was we can know only by knowing the story of which he is himself the hero – his biography, in other words; everything else we know of him, including the work he may have produced and left behind, tells us only *what* he is or was.

(HC: 186)

For Arendt, the philosophical way of defining man misses the essential question of his singularity, what it is that makes particular men particular: the who rather than the what. For Arendt, the answer to this question is found in his actions, which become meaningful when they are made into the story of his life, his biography.

Arendt cites the example of the theatre to elucidate this claim about how identity is revealed in biography. For the philosophical tradition from Plato to Marx, the theatre has symbolised the way in which man cannot know the meaning of his actions, a meaning which instead belongs to the higher force that pulls the strings behind the scenes. Arendt follows the philosophical tradition halfway, in that she agrees that the meaning of acts is not revealed to the actor. But neither, she thought, does the meaning of these acts belong to the higher force pulling the strings, the god (in Plato) or class interest (in Marx). 'Although everybody started his life by inserting himself into the human world through action and speech,' writes Arendt, 'nobody is the author or producer of his own life story' (HC: 184). This is because the meaning of our actions, the story of our life, can only be told when that life has become whole, after death. The life-story is ultimately a story that is told by others. For Arendt the meaning of action 'belongs' neither to the actor, nor to some higher force that determines the acts, but is revealed to the community that hears the story of the actor after his death.

Arendt imagines this community as the audience of a tragic drama. The theatre, for Arendt, qualifies as 'the political art par excellence' (HC: 188). This is because drama is, of all the arts, the purest imitation of human action. Where a painting makes human action into a static image, or lyric poetry makes action into a kind of 'song', drama stays closest to the reproduction of the events that it describes. For Arendt, the tragic theatre of the ancient Greeks, with its actors, audience and chorus, provides a powerful distillation of what human action really is. The hero of a Greek tragedy, such as Sophocles' King Oedipus, is blind to the meaning of his actions as they unfold, while the audience stands in the position of the gods, knowing the full story before it has even unfolded. Arendt gives a new source for the meaning of action: the community, the audience that hears different versions of the stories told about one of its members, instead of the philosopher/god who, in Plato, stands outside of human affairs.

CONCLUSION

Arendt turns the long philosophical tradition of viewing the theatre as a microcosm of the self-deception of human action upside down. The theatre becomes, instead, an image for how action and meaning might be reconciled in the community. The reconciliation takes place in the act of judging the acts portrayed on the stage. Arendt takes the meaning of action out of the transcendent realm of the gods, and gives it back to the community. This chapter has explored two contemporary bodies of thought that testify to a failure of the synthesis between thought and action proposed by Arendt's work: existential philosophy and sociology. I have also suggested that Arendt's work might offer a new way to think about philosophical questions in literary texts from a perspective that refuses to assume that any thinking and reflection in our reading leads inevitably to abstraction.

4

LABOUR, WORK AND
MODERNISM

Given that a major ambition of her work was to respond to what she perceived to be a radical break with tradition, Arendt might usefully be defined as a philosophical and political 'modernist'. This is not to say, however, that Arendt was committed in any way to 'defending' the modern world, that she believed fundamentally in ideas of progress, or that she understood modern technology and science to have liberated mankind from labour. In her book *The Reluctant Modernism of Hannah Arendt*, Seyla Benhabib writes that,

> although Hannah Arendt, the stateless person and persecuted Jew, is the
> philosophical and political modernist, Arendt, the student of Martin Heidegger,
> is the antimodernist Grecophile theorist of the *polis* and of its lost glory.
>
> (Benhabib 1996: xxiv–xxv)

This equivocal attitude towards modernity makes Arendt, in Benhabib's view, a 'reluctant' modernist. Committed to the ideal political conditions embodied by ancient Greek culture, Arendt was also aware that these conditions could never, and indeed should never, be recovered in a modern, democratic social condition. Society is not a condition that could simply be wished away through a nostalgic return to the vigorous life of the ancient Greek polis, with its sharp distinction between public and private spaces, as well as between slaves, barbarians and free men. Rather, the crucial task, for Arendt, was to understand society. Her writing explores the ways in which an understanding of modernity that takes its bearings from classical antiquity might yield a new critical perspective on the distinctively modern phenomenon of society.

A preoccupation with the relation between the ancient and modern worlds characterises a good deal of modernist writing, both literary and philosophical. This chapter will examine the question of Arendt's modernism, and in particular it will look at her critical attitude towards the dominant kinds of activity that go on in modern society, namely labour and consumerism. In order to do this, Arendt's work will be placed in the context of other modernists who look back to classical antiquity in order to critique the modern world, and in particular, to critique the distinctively modern phenomenon of mass society. The most crucial figure for Arendt in this regard was Martin Heidegger, but in what follows, her modernism will also be elucidated with reference to three modernist literary writers working in English: the novelists James Joyce (1882–1941) and Virginia Woolf (1882–1941), and the poet T.S. Eliot (1888–1965).

HEIDEGGER AND ARENDT

Heidegger is an essential figure for the understanding of Arendt's work as a whole. He is at once everywhere and nowhere in her work. *The Human Condition* never mentions Heidegger by name, yet it is crucially indebted to his ways of thinking. Shortly after the war had ended, at a time when Arendt had no personal communication with Heidegger, she wrote a very hostile account of his thought in an article called 'What is Existential Philosophy?' (1946). But apart from this article, Arendt offered no significant engagement with Heidegger's thought in print until the very end of her life, when she considered it in detail in her last, unfinished book, *The Life of the Mind*.

In interpreting Heidegger's influence on Arendt, it is important to be attentive to this silence in her work, and to understand it as imbued with meaning. This chapter will examine the ways in which Arendt was crucially enabled by Heidegger's philosophical method in the critique of society that she offers in *The Human Condition*, even though she also contested certain key aspects of Heidegger's thinking. To this extent, it will read *The Human Condition* as a critical negotiation with Heidegger that operates through silence, by never engaging with him directly. This is an area of Arendt's thought that has been well documented by Arendt scholars (Hinchman and Hinchman 1984; Benhabib 1996; Villa 1996). In particular, *The Human Condition* has been read as an attempt to offer a politicised version of Heidegger's philosophy. Heidegger's own relation to politics is complex. According to Benhabib, the 'path to the political' in Heidegger 'is opened up and closed off' (Benhabib 1996: 53). One way of reading *The Human Condition* is as an attempt to open up again that political path, to see through to fruition the full political potential of Heidegger's philosophy.

HEIDEGGER, DEATH AND THE SELF

In 'What is Existential Philosophy?', Arendt described the central problem with Heidegger's thought to be its preoccupation with the category of the self. 'The essential character of the Self', writes Arendt, 'is its absolute Self-ness, its radical separation from all its fellows' (EU: 181). One reason why the self is isolated in Heidegger's thought is because it is faced with the anticipation of its own death. According to Heidegger, the self that does not hide from the real meaning of its existence will know that it has to die one day. But Heidegger thought of everyday existence as a condition in which the self becomes 'forgetful' of the fact of its own impending death. According to Heidegger, the modern self actively cultivates this forgetfulness by immersing itself in the company of others. In company, it becomes easy to evade a meaningful awareness of death. In his book *Being and Time* (1927), Heidegger writes:

> In the publicness with which we are with one another in our everyday manner, death is 'known' as a mishap which is constantly occurring – as a 'case of death' [...] 'Death' is encountered as a well-known event occurring within-the-world. As such it remains in the inconspicuousness characteristic of what is encountered in an everyday fashion.
>
> (Heidegger 1967: 296–97)

According to Heidegger, the public world allows death to become an everyday fact. By belonging to a group, the self is able to form an everyday, social idea of death, which allows that self to evade a real awareness of its own impending death. Through social conventions such as funeral rights and a euphemistic language for talking about the death of others (in English we might say that someone has 'passed on' or that we have 'lost' them) death becomes something that always happens to other people. Heidegger wanted to penetrate through this inauthentic, everyday and public understanding of death. He argues that, contrary to this everyday understanding of death, the reality of death belongs to the self. 'By its very essence, death is in every case mine, in so far as it 'is' at all' (Heidegger 1967: 284).

Clearly, for Heidegger, the individual rather than the community is the real source of meaning, particularly as he searches for the meaning of fundamental life experiences such as death. For Heidegger, if death is understood in an authentic way, it creates a crisis for the community of those who survive the death of someone else. Heidegger argues that we can find evidence of this crisis in the experiences of grief and mourning. Since the self can never, in truth, experience the death of the other, that death gives a shocking sense of separation and loss to the self. Heidegger argues that the death of someone else 'is not something which we experience in a genuine sense; at most we are always just "there alongside"' (Heidegger 1967: 282). Awareness of the death of others affirms the self, to paraphrase Arendt, in its condition of 'absolute Self-ness' and its 'separation from all its fellows'.

In *The Human Condition*, by contrast, Arendt understands the death of the self as an event that gives the meaning of a life back to the community to which that self had belonged, enabling that community to make a coherent narrative out of it (see Chapters 2 and 3). Death, in other words, is not a point of isolation and loneliness for Arendt, nor does it generate what Heidegger describes as the 'idle talk' of the public realm (Heidegger 1967: 296). For Arendt, rather, death signals the possibility of public communication, and the beginning of a story.

CASE STUDY 4: ELIOT AND WOOLF

Might Arendt and Heidegger's different attitudes to death be understood in terms of the differences between writing by men and women in the modernist period? The different attitudes to death in Arendt and Heidegger compare well to the differences between two English modernist writers, one male and one female, for whom death is an equally important theme. In his 1922 poem *The Waste Land*, T.S. Eliot describes a crowd of commuters going to work in London.

Unreal City
Under the brown fog of a winter dawn
A crowd flowed over London Bridge, so many,
I had not thought death had undone so many.
Sighs, short and infrequent, were exhaled,
And each man fixed his eyes before his feet.
(Eliot 1990: 25)

A few years later, in 1925, the heroine of Virginia Woolf's novel *Mrs Dalloway* reflects on the suicide of a shell-shocked First World War veteran, Septimus Warren Smith, in the following way.

Death was defiance. Death was an attempt to communicate, people feeling the impossibility of reaching the centre which, mystically, evaded them; closeness drew apart; rapture faded; one was alone. There was an embrace in death.
(Woolf 2000: 202)

Eliot's street scene describes a group of commuters, on their way to work, isolated from one another with their eyes fixed before their feet, undone by death. The notion of death here might be taken to indicate the level of solitude and conformism evident in modern society, and in particular in the modern social phenomenon of the crowd. For Eliot as for Heidegger, this is a social condition which actively cultivates a state of forgetfulness around death ('I had not thought death had undone so many'). For Woolf, by contrast, the death of a young war veteran is a kind of creative act, an act of resistance or defiance. While we are alone in death, and in thinking about death, death can also be an attempt to communicate. It can signal a positive insight into our failure to see into the centre of things. Similarly, for Arendt, the death of a hero inspires togetherness and the possibility of communication.

COMMUNITY

In *The Human Condition*, Arendt seeks to give a sense of authenticity to collective, political life, and to the condition of human plurality, that is denied to it by Heidegger. The path to the political in Heidegger is blocked by his suspicious attitude towards public human togetherness. In a post-war work, the 'Letter on Humanism' (1947), Heidegger refers to 'the peculiar dictatorship of the public realm' (Heidegger 1993: 221). Arendt's work, by contrast, is centrally preoccupied with the effort to make of the public realm a space of freedom.

The relationship between Arendt and Heidegger is, however, a finer one than contrast. Their conflicting understanding of the relation between self and community tells only half the story. It leaves unexplained the crucial and fundamental ways in which Heidegger's work enabled Arendt's critique of modern society. In particular, Arendt thought that Heidegger's work opened up the possibility of a way of thinking about the world that overcame both the excuses made by social democracy for a crushing social conformism and the false, world-alienating promise of a revolutionised society offered by Marxism. What Heidegger's thought offered her was a fundamentally new way of looking at the human condition, and the possibility of tracing the historical development of a culture that has lost touch with the reality of that condition.

HEIDEGGER AND THE PHILOSOPHICAL TRADITION

Arendt was deeply influenced by Heidegger's effort to depart from the philosophical tradition. Because of this effort, Heidegger's writing, like Arendt's, can seem strange on first encounter. This strangeness is a quality of its attempt to abandon dominant habits of thinking which, according to Heidegger, have led modern man into a condition of 'forgetfulness' and 'rootlessness'. On first reading Heidegger's essays, one has the sense of leaving the known domain of philosophical tradition, and tracking out across an unfamiliar landscape. A sense of the disorienting effect of Heidegger's writing can be found in his essay 'The Origin of the Work of Art', which was first given as a series of lectures in 1935–36, during the period of Arendt's estrangement from him, but was published in German in 1950, one year before they recommenced their friendship:

> We believe we are at home in the immediate circle of beings. Beings are familiar, reliable, ordinary. Nevertheless, the clearing is pervaded by a constant concealment in the double form of refusal and dissembling. At bottom, the ordinary is not ordinary; it is extraordinary.

(Heidegger 1993: 179)

Leaving aside the peculiar use of terms such as 'clearing' and 'being', it seems from the tone of this passage that Heidegger wants to challenge the certainty by which man feels at home in the world. He wants to suggest that, if we can learn to look at them in a different way, things that seem 'ordinary' to us are revealed as actually being, 'at bottom', extraordinary and uncanny. Part of this extraordinariness is to do with the way in which things refuse to tell us what they really are, or the way in which they dissemble what they really are.

Heidegger writes in the same essay that 'What seems natural to us is probably just something familiar in a long tradition that has forgotten the unfamiliar source from which it arose' (Heidegger 1993: 150). The effort to 'remember' this source for our everyday perception of things, and thereby to challenge the status of that perception as natural, involves Heidegger in a 'deep' historical analysis. This analysis draws attention to how dominant habits of understanding and perceiving the world have been shaped in a particular way by the historical culture that we inhabit. Heidegger takes the languages of the West to be sedimented with a record of how this shaped understanding has developed in Europe, and so linguistic analysis is a crucial part of Heidegger's 'deep history'. Essentially, by tracing some developments in language use and grammar, Heidegger thinks that he can show how an originally harmonious relationship between man and the world around him has become distorted over time.

Heidegger pays attention, in his essay on the work of art, to the way in which ancient Greek concepts, and with them the ancient Greek understanding of the relation between man and the world, were translated into equivalent terms in ancient Latin. This act of translation sees a more harmonious relation between man and the world in Greek culture prior to Plato and Aristotle (who prepared the ground for the modern world) replaced by a kind of non-relation. Heidegger argues that the Roman, unlike the Greek, understood the world around him, and the things in that world, to exist for the purposes of his use and exploitation. In the new attitude developed by the Romans, which involved 'violence' towards things (Heidegger 1993: 150), man became so preoccupied with the question of how the things that he finds around him in the world might be useful to him that he forgot to think about what those things might be in and for themselves. The Latin language, and in particular the grammar of the Latin sentence, argues Heidegger, shows evidence of how for the Romans the things of the world – its objects – were understood to exist only in relation to the human self – the subject. Heidegger writes that 'this translation of Greek names into Latin is in no way the innocent process it is considered to this day', but that rather 'The rootlessness of Western thought begins with this translation' (Heidegger 1993: 149).

A preoccupation with translation is also an important aspect of *The Human Condition*. For example, where Heidegger thinks about an act of translation between Greek and Latin, Arendt thinks about one between Latin and modern English. Arendt thinks about how the modern English word 'private' takes over the meaning of the Latin word *privatus*, but loses touch with the experience that, for the Romans, went with this word.

> In ancient feeling the privative trait of privacy, indicated in the word itself, was all-important; it meant literally a state of being deprived of something, even of the highest and most human of man's capacities […] We no longer think primarily of deprivation when we use the word "privacy," and this is partly due to the enormous enrichment of the private sphere through modern individualism.
>
> (HC: 38)

In modern culture, we may feel that the private is the 'primary' or 'first' category of our experience, such that we imagine ourselves going out *from* private space *into* the public. For example, we find ourselves in the private world of the home and the family at the beginning of our lives, and then at some point we decide to move out into the public realm. But Arendt shows with this analysis of the word 'private' that things were once the other way around. 'Private', for the Romans, suggested that something was being taken away – and Arendt shows that we can hear an echo of this original meaning in another word with the same root, 'deprivation'. The point here is that, in the ancient world, privacy was a secondary state to the public, and it involved some kind of loss, pain or deprivation of 'the highest and most human of man's capacities'. We in the modern world, however, tend to value the private realm of leisure time, the home and family attachment over any sense of public identity we might have. There has been an 'enormous enrichment', Arendt says, of the private sphere through 'modern individualism' – and, we might infer from this, a similarly enormous impoverishment of the public sphere, where modern man tends to appear as a job holder, someone who is perhaps alienated from his work, and who suffers a sense of deprivation on leaving his home.

For both Arendt and Heidegger, linguistic analysis shows up the modern condition as one of 'rootlessness'. Language has the power to disclose how certain aspects of modern experience, which may seem familiar and 'normal' to us, are in fact the result of a distortion or mistranslation of the experience of the cultures of ancient Greece and Rome. For both Arendt and Heidegger, looking at language in this way has the power to make the familiar world around us suddenly seem strange and unfamiliar.

LABOUR

In *The Human Condition*, Arendt applies this kind of phenomenological analysis to the type of human activity that she takes to define modern social experience: labour. Arendt's analysis of the labouring activity suspends any assumptions that we might have about it, and the dominant modern theoretical treatment it has received in Marxism, in favour of applying the definition of labour found in ancient Greek theory to contemporary society. In particular, Arendt seeks to distinguish labour as one of three fundamental types of human activity, the others being work and action.

Arendt points out that Aristotle defines labour in his *Politics* as the activity by which 'slaves and tame animals with their bodies minister to the necessities of life' (HC: 80). Since labour is undertaken by both men and animals, labour is, in Aristotle's theory, the least distinctively human of man's activities. As the activity of slaves and animals, labour is, according to Aristotle, the type of activity that is most closely associated with the body. This association also binds labour up with necessity and with privacy – and therefore, as we have just seen, with the pain of deprivation. According to Greek political theory, it is in the private realm of the *oikos* that man's physical, bodily needs are administered to (see Chapter 2). The association of labour with the body and with necessity also means that, in Arendt's view, the labouring activity is essentially continuous with the natural world. She claims that labour perpetuates 'the unceasing, indefatigable cycle in which the whole household of nature swings perpetually' (HC: 97).

Arendt does not want to do away with labour altogether. She claims rather that there has always been, and always will be, labour in human societies, and that it is an important part of the human condition. But whereas in the ancient world, labour took place in the strictly bounded and delimited setting of the *oikos* or household, in the modern world it has become the dominant *public* activity. Arendt's argument about labour is then a part of her larger argument about society (see Chapter 2) in that Arendt understands the dominance of labour in modern society as evidence of a private activity taking over the public realm. Arendt writes that as long as *animal laborans*, or man as a labouring animal, 'remains in possession of it, there can be no true public realm, but only private activities displayed in the open' (HC: 134). Arendt thinks of public space as a space of human togetherness. The invasion of this space by the labouring activity, the making of labourers into the primary public agents, is catastrophic, since the labourer is bound up in an essentially 'natural' or metabolic relationship with his body, and therefore can form no real political bonds with others. Rather, labouring, as a fully social relation, condemns the labourer to a condition of 'imprisonment within the self' (HC: 168).

Arendt's argument could be made to seem highly reactionary – to boil down to a claim that the visibility of exploited workers in industrial and so-called 'post-industrial' societies is unseemly, and serves only to interrupt the properly public and patrician activities of political dialogue and persuasion. In fact it claims no such thing. To get to grips with Arendt's argument, it is important to bear in mind that, following Heidegger, she understands labour phenomenologically, rather than in purely empirical, historical terms. In other words, she is interested in labour as a type of human activity, and in what it tells us about the relation between man and the world, rather than in offering any historically factual account of particular labourers. Indeed, Arendt does not think, as we might assume, that the 'labourer' is synonymous with the working classes of industrialised societies. Rather, she writes that modern society did not come about 'through the emancipation of the laboring classes but by the emancipation of the laboring activity itself' (HC: 126). In modern societies, the emancipation of labour from its ancient restriction to the home means we are nearly all labourers, according to Arendt's fundamental definition of labour.

CONSUMERISM

Arendt claims that in our society, public space is increasingly organised around the satisfaction of private needs and the achievement of comfort. This modern social condition condemns most of the population to a life where they suffer dissatisfaction and loneliness. The social self divides his or her time between labour – the production of commodities – and the private consumption of commodities, but has no opportunity to participate in common, public life. Therefore a 'postmodern culture' based around the consumption of commodities, rather than large-scale industrial production, is still modelled for Arendt on the image of the labourer. Labour, for her, is bound up with consumption as the two halves of a metabolic cycle that defines modern society. These are, Arendt claims, 'but two stages of the ever-recurring cycle of biological life. This cycle needs to be sustained through consumption, and the activity which provides the means of consumption is laboring' (HC: 99).

CASE STUDY 5: ARENDT, JOYCE AND CONSUMPTION

Arendt illustrates the cyclical nature of this relationship by analogy with the literal act of consumption – eating. Arendt writes that labour and eating are both 'devouring processes that seize and destroy matter' (HC: 100). Matter is reproduced in the course of these two activities, in the form of commodities that are designed to be thrown away and turned into waste in the case of labour, and excrement in the case of eating. The process is then cyclical: labour and eating seize and devour matter in order to produce more matter, which can then be seized again and so on. Arendt understands modern social activity, by analogy with bodily processes, as essentially a 'waste economy' (HC: 134).

A preoccupation with waste and consumption runs throughout modernist writing. In the 'Lestrygonians' episode of James Joyce's epic novel *Ulysses* (1922), Joyce's hero Leopold Bloom juxtaposes thoughts about the classical ideal of artistic beauty with an awareness of the human body and its material needs. Bloom's reverie begins with him looking at the shape of the bar in a pub where he is having lunch:

> His downcast eyes followed the silent veining of the oaken slab. Beauty: it curves: curves are beauty. Shapely goddesses, Venus, Juno: curves the world admires […] Lovely forms of woman sculped Junonian. Immortal lovely. And

we stuffing food in one hole and out behind: food, chyle, blood, dung, earth, food: have to feed it like stoking an engine.

(Joyce 1998: 168)

For Bloom, beauty becomes synonymous with the female form, and in particular the form of ancient goddesses as it is represented in classical sculpture. This ideal form is contrasted with the body of 'we' – presumably both mortals and men – for whom the body has become a kind of machine. This machine is trapped in the same metabolic relationship with nature that Arendt describes in the labouring activity. Food is processed and given back to the earth as dung, from which it springs forth again as food. Matter is moving in a continual cycle, and is juxtaposed, by Joyce, with the 'immortal lovely' of the female form. Curiously enough, both the immortal form of the goddess and the cyclical, metabolic body of the mortal man are versions of nature: one is an image of an ideal, intellectual beauty found in nature, the other figures nature as a repetitive machine. This contrast between two different ways of imagining nature – as immortal form versus endless process – also helps to define the key difference between Arendt and Heidegger in their respective engagements with the work of art.

THE WORK OF ART

In *The Human Condition*, Arendt tries to recover a classical definition of work as a specific form of human activity. Arendt thinks that labour has become so ubiquitous in modern society that it has swallowed up 'work', which, before the rise of modern society, was a type of activity that was thoroughly distinct from labour. It is worth looking at her argument about work in some detail because it discloses Arendt's sense of the importance of art in the modern world. The work of art, for Arendt, is the last remaining product of human activity in modernity that has remained distinct from labour, the last human product that is not a commodity. Art then opens up the possibility of imagining a different way of life, which is not predicated on the loneliness, unhappiness and sheer physical exertion of the labourer/consumer.

As with labour, Arendt is preoccupied with offering a phenomenology of work. If labour produces nothing and is essentially continuous with nature, giving back the matter which it takes from it, then the main characteristics of work are that it transforms nature and produces things which have durability and value. Where labour is primarily a form of activity that involves the whole human body in a 'metabolism' with nature, work involves the dexterity of hands and of tools. It uses these to take its raw material from nature and to transform it through the process of fabrication. This transformation takes the raw material out of the natural cycle and, by shaping it into a different form, gives it some degree of permanence. Where labour is essentially an isolated and lonely condition, in which man is involved in a relationship with his body, work already presupposes a community and public space, in that it produces durable objects which can appear in the marketplace and be exchanged. Since work is bound up with fabrication, it also builds a durable and stable home for man in the world. The products of work 'give the human artifice the stability and solidity without which it could not be relied upon to house the unstable and mortal creature which is man' (HC: 136). In essence, Arendt argues that work builds the world of human culture.

WORLD AND EARTH IN HEIDEGGER

Here again, Arendt's argument can be productively compared with Heidegger's in his essay 'The Origin of the Work of Art'. For Heidegger, the work of art makes space for the world in nature. Heidegger makes the same distinction as Arendt between nature and the world as a human artifice. 'A stone is worldless', he writes. 'Plant and animal likewise have no world'; however, 'To work-being there belongs the setting up of a world' (Heidegger 1993: 171). What is important about the work of art, for Heidegger, is that it effects a reconciliation between the world and nature, or the 'earth' as Heidegger calls it. For the 'metaphysical' tradition of thought and language inherited by the modern world from the Romans, according to Heidegger, the natural world, or the 'earth', has seemed to exist solely for the benefit of man. But in the making of works of art, Heidegger finds a possible model for a different relationship between the world of human culture and nature, one that does not rest on man's violent, appropriative tendencies. Heidegger gives an example for this relationship between earth and world from the field of architecture. An ancient Greek temple, he claims, reconciles culture and nature, world and earth; 'The temple-work, standing there, opens up a world and at the same time sets this world back again on earth, which itself only thus emerges as native ground' (Heidegger 1993: 168).

As a work of art, the temple brings forth the relation between the earth and the world. It discloses the way that the world that opens itself to the human self rests on a natural earth. But the relationship is two-way: this earth 'emerges', its identity is disclosed, through its support for the world. The relationship is symbiotic and not violent: the 'world' of civilisation represented by the temple allows the earth to shine forth as the earth. The earth exists in harmony with the human work that has gone into the production of the temple. As Heidegger summarises: '*The work lets the earth be an earth*' (Heidegger 1993: 172).

ARENDT AND THE WORK OF ART

Given her largely hostile attitude towards the natural world, it is difficult to imagine Arendt thinking in quite the same ecological terms as Heidegger about the relationship between the world and nature. For Arendt, 'work' involves precisely the kind of violent attitude towards nature that Heidegger seeks to overcome. She writes of 'the tree which must be destroyed in order to provide wood', and of 'iron, stone or marble torn out of the womb of the earth' (HC: 139). Because of her assumption that society is an unnatural 'outgrowth of the natural', Arendt understands nature as a dark and dangerous force that must be continually overpowered by man.

The chief characteristic of the work of art, for Arendt, is that it has durability. The work of art exists through time, often for centuries, and so it escapes the natural cycle of labour and consumption. Works of art 'are the most intensely worldly of all tangible things; their durability is almost untouched by the corroding effect of natural processes' (HC: 167). Arendt thinks of stories as kinds of work. 'Action', she writes, "produces" stories with or without intention as naturally as fabrication produces tangible things' (HC: 184). Taking action as its raw material, the story 'works' on action in order to give it durability and remembrance.

The story challenges the dominant Western paradigm for understanding action offered by the philosophical tradition. Despite the radical abandonment of tradition proposed by his work, according to

Arendt, Heidegger still maintained the superior pose that thought has traditionally taken over action. This is a fairly paradoxical claim for Arendt to make, given Heidegger's desire to escape the violence of traditional philosophy. But it is born out by 'The Origin of the Work of Art':

> Thinking towers above action and production, not through the grandeur of its achievement and not as a consequence of its effect, but through the humbleness of its inconsequential accomplishment.
>
> (Heidegger 1993: 262)

Symptomatically, in towering over action and production, thinking fails to consider what might be at stake in the distinction it makes between them.

CONCLUSION

In its lofty attitude towards action, theory has historically failed to pay attention to the distinctions between the different types of human activity, labour, work and action. The whole of *The Human Condition* can then be understood as an archaeological effort to recover meaningful distinctions between these different, fundamental types of human activity. This chapter has considered the question of Arendt's modernism, in the contexts of her relation to Heidegger and her account in *The Human Condition* of labour and work as distinct types of activity. It has shown how Arendt and Heidegger differ in fundamental ways on two issues: public space, which for Heidegger is a sphere of 'idle talk' and which for Arendt appears the only real path to human freedom; and the work of art, which for Heidegger brings about a reconciliation between 'world' and 'earth', whereas for Arendt 'work' transforms nature in the building of a human world. This chapter has also discussed Arendt's phenomenology of labour and consumerism, the types of activity that in Arendt's view have become dominant in the modern world. Finally, it was suggested that for Arendt, Heidegger is not sufficiently distant from the philosophical tradition inaugurated by Plato.

5

JUDGING: FROM KANT TO EICHMANN

Rose is a rose is a rose
Gertrude Stein, 'Sacred Emily' (1922)

This chapter will bring together two areas of Arendt's thought which may at first sight appear to have very little in common. It will consider her interpretation of the work of the Enlightenment philosopher Immanuel Kant (1724–1804), and in particular a series of lectures that Arendt gave in 1970 on Kant's book *Critique of Judgement* (1790) at the New School for Social Research in New York. Blended together with this attention to Arendt's reading of Kant, this chapter will also begin to consider Arendt's work on totalitarian rule in Germany, and in particular her effort to think about the Holocaust, by examining her book *Eichmann in Jerusalem: A Report on the Banality of Evil* (1963). Arendt's lectures on a book by Kant which is concerned with questions about art and beauty, and her writing on the trial of a former member of the SS, may seem to have very little to do with each other. Not only that, but it may even seem to be distasteful to juxtapose the study of artistic beauty with questions about the Nazi genocide against the Jews. Arendt's account of totalitarian rule, and of the trial of Adolf Eichmann in particular, was controversial, and did seem distasteful and tactless to a number of her contemporary readers, as it still does to some readers today (Ceserani 2007). Yet Arendt was not alone in thinking about the Holocaust in the context of issues about artistic beauty. Her contemporary, the critical theorist Theodor Adorno, famously argued in an essay published in the same year as *The Origins of Totalitarianism*, 1951, that to write poetry after Auschwitz is 'barbaric' (Adorno 2003: 281). What is it that brings together two such different topics as the Holocaust and the status of art in modernity?

THE PROBLEM OF JUDGEMENT

Arendt's writings on Immanuel Kant and Adolf Eichmann share a preoccupation with the problem of judgement. In the *Critique of Judgement*, Kant set out to analyse what happens when someone judges a particular thing – say, a poem, a painting, a song, or a landscape – to be beautiful. In a very different way, the court in Jerusalem that put Eichmann on trial in 1961 set out to make a judgement of his actions during the Second World War, and in particular to determine his responsibility for the genocide committed against the Jewish people in Europe. Although these two forms of judgement clearly differ from one another in important respects, in Arendt's writing they overlap and encounter similar problems, and ultimately become mutually informative. In considering the trial of Eichmann and the philosophy of Kant, Arendt engaged with a problem that has defined modern critical thought, and indeed modern international relations, in a central way: the problem of what justice means in a world which has shed all absolute notions of 'truth', and in a world which has witnessed unparalleled horror in the total domination of human beings by totalitarian states.

THE EICHMANN TRIAL

During the Second World War, Adolf Eichmann had been responsible for organising the enormously complex railroad transportation of Jews from the German Reich to the concentration camps in the east. Israeli secret agents had kidnapped him from outside his home in Buenos Aires, Argentina, in 1960 and taken him to Israel, where he was put on trial for crimes against the Jewish people. There were a number of legal problems with this trial. Israel had violated international law and Argentinean sovereignty by kidnapping Eichmann, which rendered the trial illegal in some people's eyes. For others, notably the philosopher Karl Jaspers, the crimes committed by the

Nazis against the Jews were in fact crimes against humanity, and so Eichmann should, Jaspers thought, be put on trial by an international court. Arendt considered these objections to be fairly insignificant. But although she condoned both the right of Israel to put Eichmann on trial and the guilty verdict that the court eventually reached, Arendt had many serious misgivings about the conduct of the trial itself, and the rationale behind it. In particular, she argued that the court had failed to face up to the challenge of judging the unprecedented nature of Eichmann's crimes.

Arendt thought that the crimes committed by the Nazis had shattered the very foundations of justice in the Western world, and that they therefore called for a rethinking of what it means to judge crime and criminality. She writes in *Eichmann in Jerusalem* of how the judges had misread the case of Eichmann:

> They preferred to conclude from occasional lies that [Eichmann] was a liar – and missed the greatest moral and even legal challenge of the whole case. Their case rested on the assumption that the defendant, like all "normal persons", must have been aware of the criminal nature of his acts, and indeed Eichmann was normal insofar as he was "no exception within the Nazi regime". However, under the conditions of the Third Reich only "exceptions" could be expected to react "normally". This simple truth of the matter created a dilemma for the judges which they could neither resolve nor escape.

(EJ: 26–27)

The problem that Eichmann presented to the court was that he did not think about the fact that he was participating in a terrible crime by organising the transportation of millions of people to their deaths. Eichmann did not act as any putatively 'normal person' would have done in his situation (in this, Arendt argues, he was a typical subject of the Nazi regime). Eichmann consistently defended himself during the trial by claiming that he had always carried out his duty to the letter – as if the court would recognise this commitment to his duty as a virtue. According to Arendt, Eichmann simply did not know – or rather, he was incapable of thinking about – the criminality of his acts, even though that criminality seems obvious to anyone who thinks about it. How could this be so?

Arendt argued in *The Origins of Totalitarianism* that the period of totalitarian rule in Germany under Hitler had effected a radical change in human nature (see Chapter 8). In particular, it was Arendt's view that life in the Nazi state had effectively destroyed the personality, the unique human identity, of men like Eichmann. A judge can only reach a guilty verdict in a court of law on the assumption that the accused was aware of what they were doing when they acted in a criminal way. If the accused is judged to be insane, for example, they are found not to be guilty of the crime on the grounds of diminished responsibility. The question of guilt, in other words, is closely tied in with the question of personal responsibility. Someone is found guilty on the assumption that they were aware of the meaning of what they were doing when they acted in a criminal way, or in other words, on the assumption that they had a conscience – an innate sense of the difference between right and wrong – even if they did not act on it. Arendt thought that Eichmann had undergone such a radical loss of his identity as an autonomous human agent, and such a radical loss of conscience, that it had become impossible to find him guilty as charged. This is not to say, however, that Arendt wanted to defend Eichmann as innocent either. Nor did she think him insane; he had been examined by Israeli psychiatrists after he was kidnapped and declared sane (Arendt claims that one of these psychiatrists declared that Eichmann was '[m]ore normal, at any rate, than I am after having examined him' (EJ: 25)). Arendt's point was that, in destroying the freedom and spontaneity of the human personality, totalitarianism had in effect destroyed the possibility of making moral and legal judgements as they had existed in Europe for centuries prior to totalitarian rule. To this extent, the unbearable crimes committed by totalitarian regimes called for a rethinking of the very idea of justice, and of personal responsibility.

Arendt's preoccupation with the issue of judgement might be phrased in the form of a question: How are we to find meaningful standards of justice and morality in a post-totalitarian and 'postmetaphysical' world in which all absolute standards of truth and goodness have collapsed? Arendt found Kant to be helpful in her effort to answer this question. For Arendt, the kinds of insight that Kant, writing in the late eighteenth century, had gleaned about the nature of aesthetic judgement, or the judgement of the beautiful, held resources that could help to get to grips with the problem for legal and moral judgement that Eichmann posed to the court in Jerusalem. Arendt found in Kant's philosophy crucial resources for thinking about unprecedented historical events and experiences, for which no theoretical, moral or historical framework for understanding exists. For Kant, the judgement of artistic or natural beauty is precisely one such experience. This is because judgement is, as Arendt quotes Kant, 'the faculty of thinking the particular' (LKPP: 76). Because Kant's treatment of judgement held such crucial resources for thinking about the problem of justice in a post-metaphysical world, Arendt thought him to be one of only very few philosophers in history to have stepped outside the 'world alienating' philosophical tradition (see Chapter 2), and to have offered a genuine philosophical reflection on the issue of human plurality. To that extent, Arendt thought that Kant's treatment of aesthetic judgement offered the groundwork for a genuine 'political philosophy'.

BEAUTY, TEACHING AND LITERARY CRITICISM

Why is Kant's interest in beauty so crucial for Arendt, and why on earth should anyone studying literature or cultural studies take an interest in it? My experience of teaching English literature has been that the question of beauty only ever arises in seminar discussion as a problem or an embarrassment. If I declare that I find a particular poem beautiful, the seminar dialogue is stopped in its tracks because I seem to be offering an entirely subjective viewpoint with which it is difficult to argue in any critical way. In declaring the poem beautiful, I seem to be making an evaluative judgement, simply asserting something about the quality of the poem, rather than opening up a critical debate about it. To this extent, the question of our appreciation for the beauty of the literary texts that we read appears to be outside the sphere of our interest as literary critics. Literary criticism, surely, should be preoccupied with trying to understand how literature comments on society, rather than in naively asserting the beauty of literary writing.

For Kant, the issue of beauty is in fact closely tied in with questions about society. An appreciation for the beautiful things that we find around us – works of art, statues, poems, music, as well as the beauty of nature – has the power to make us feel at home in the world. It therefore goes against the 'world alienation' of the philosophical tradition (see Chapter 1). An interest in the beautiful, according to Kant, can flourish only in society. In her lectures on Kant, Arendt quotes him to this effect:

> [T]he beautiful interests [us] only [when we are] in society ... A man aban-
> doned by himself on a desert island would adorn neither his hut nor his
> person ... [Man] is not contented with an object if he cannot feel satisfaction
> in it in common with others.
>
> (LKPP: 67)

According to Kant, an appreciation for beauty, while it strikes the individual, also fits him for society, since he wants to communicate his experience of beauty to others. It is almost impossible to imagine anyone being interested in beauty, argues Kant, if they were not in society, if for instance like Robinson Crusoe they lived alone on a desert island. The question of beauty, for Arendt and Kant, is actually about far more than our judgement of works of art. Rather, it takes such judgements to offer crucial information both about what society is and about how man is a fundamentally sociable being. Arendt was much more interested in these questions about man's sociability in her lectures on Kant than she was interested in questions about beauty.

IMAGINATION

In her report on the Eichmann trial, Arendt showed that it was precisely those aspects of social identity that are associated with the judgement of beauty that Eichmann had lost. Most importantly, she thought, Eichmann was lacking in any 'imagination'. Since the Romantic period, writers and philosophers have described how the imagination plays an important role in our appreciation for artworks, and how it also makes up a crucial part of our social identity. The imagination allows us to think about – or rather, to imagine – how the world appears from someone else's point of view. In a postscript to her book on the Eichmann trial, Arendt identified a 'lack of imagination' that 'enabled [Eichmann] to sit for months on end facing a German Jew who was conducting the police interrogation, pouring out his heart to the man and explaining again and again how it was that he reached only the rank of lieutenant colonel in the SS and that it had not been his fault that he was not promoted' (EJ: 287). Eichmann's lack of imagination meant that he was oblivious to the fact that a German Jew might have very little sympathy for his complaints about the dif-ficulties he had had in advancing his career in the SS. Imagination is bound up for Arendt with the power of empathy – the power to think about things from someone else's point of view. This is a power that was obviously lacking in Eichmann, judging by his tactlessness.

In her lectures on Kant, Arendt demonstrates much more expansively how the power of imagination allows individuals to escape from the confines of their selfhood, and to think from the point of view of others. She writes of how Kant 'stresses that at least one of our *mental faculties*, the faculty of judgment, presupposes the presence of others' (LKPP: 74). In making judgements of the beautiful, as Kant puts it, 'we must renounce ourselves in favor of others'. He also claims that in the activity of judging 'egoism is overcome' (LKPP: 67).

What might Kant mean by these extraordinary claims? Essentially, Kant claims that the judgement of beauty allows us to overcome what is most private and incommunicable about our experience of the world – that is, the experience of the world that comes to us from our bodily senses. In his book *The Ideology of the Aesthetic*, Terry Eagleton describes the social ambitions of Kant's theory of judgement in the following way:

> In the sphere of aesthetic culture [...] we can experience our shared humanity with all the immediacy of our response to a fine painting or a magnificent symphony. Paradoxically, it is in the apparently most private, frail and intangible aspects of our lives that we blend most harmoniously with one another.
>
> (Eagleton 1990: 76)

There is a central paradox at the heart of our appreciation of art, according to Eagleton. Our response to art involves a certain 'immediacy'. We are struck by beauty in an immediate, inner and totally subjective way. But through this private and immediate experience, we are able to share in a common sense of 'humanity' with others. The experience of finding something beautiful seems to strike us as individuals and as members of a group at the same time.

CASE STUDY 6: IMAGINATION, SOCIETY AND THE BODY

Kant's claim about how in judgements of beauty 'egoism is overcome' might be clarified by analogy with a modernist literary text. Stephen Dedalus, the semi-autobiographical hero of James Joyce's *A Portrait of the Artist as a Young Man* (1916) makes a distinction between 'proper' and 'improper' art, in order to explain why some artworks give us the experience of beauty while others do not:

> The feelings excited by improper art are kinetic, desire or loathing. Desire urges us to possess, to go to something; loathing urges us to abandon, to go from something. The arts which excite them, pornographical or didactic, are therefore improper arts. The esthetic emotion (I use the general term) is therefore static. The mind is arrested and raised above desire or loathing.
>
> (Joyce 1996: 233)

According to Stephen Dedalus, if we are sexually aroused by an image, say a pornographic image, or if an image is intended to make us act in a certain way, such as a piece of advertising or a piece of government propaganda, we cannot have a real aesthetic judgement of the image, because our desire, our bodily sense, is at work. The liking for the beautiful has to be, by contrast, what Dedalus calls 'static' and what Kant calls 'disinterested'. Like Stephen Dedalus, Kant claims that, as long as we are using our bodily senses to make a judgement, we are in some way 'involved' with the object, by desiring it or by being motivated by it. In order to form judgements of the beautiful we need instead to purify our response to the object of anything partial or subjective, anything that might derive from our senses or from the 'egotism' of our natural, bodily self. In order to attain this disinterested state, Kant claims that we need to use our power of imagination. The imagination releases us, temporarily, from the particular, bodily standpoint that we occupy in the world, and allows us to think from a more general standpoint. This ability to be transported out of ourselves also means that we are able to overcome our partial prejudices and motivations, and therefore to gain a 'disinterested' awareness of beauty. The key point for Arendt is that, in attaining this 'disinterested' state, we are fitted into a community. We overcome the private, subjective natural self in an experience of beauty that fits us together with others in a common culture.

ENLARGED THOUGHT

Arendt's term for the attainment of this disinterested perspective is 'enlarged thought' or 'enlarged mentality'. It is almost as if the individual mind, in the operation of judgement, expands and takes into account the views of others. The setting aside of egoistic, private or bodily interests allows the individual to cultivate what Arendt describes as 'a general standpoint, the impartiality the Judge is supposed to exercise when he lays down his verdict' (LKPP: 56). Of course, in reality, no one can ever fully set aside their egoistic self and its desires, its preferences and things that it finds repellent. To do so would be to disown one's own body. But there are certain types of judging experience which encourage us to set aside our 'private' self and our inclinations and to take up a more objective standpoint.

JUDGING DRAMA

Arendt's example of impartiality in judgement is the audience or spectator of a play:

> The advantage the spectator has is that he sees the play as a whole, while each of the actors knows only his part or, if he should judge from the perspective of acting, only the part of the whole that concerns him. The actor is partial by definition.

(LKPP: 68–69)

According to Arendt, we can never adequately judge our own actions because we cannot gain the necessary detachment from those acts that would be required to understand their full real meaning. What we do in our lives often has repercussions that we do not and cannot know about (for example, what we have done may influence the lives of others after our death) and so we can never know the full meaning of our actions. We are, in a sense, acting a part in a larger drama in living our lives. We can, however, judge the acts of others, as we might judge the acts of particular characters in a play. Yet while a spectator 'sees the play as a whole', her perspective is not fully abstracted from the action. She does not see things objectively, because she remains absorbed by the spectacle. The spectator or audience member is involved in the play – a crucial part of it, since the play is not a play without her – but she also stands outside the action, and can see its whole meaning. The spectator's imagination allows her to identify with the actors on the stage. The spectator's emotions are her own, but they respond to the portrayal of someone else's emotional life, or in the case of a tragedy, of someone else's suffering.

'SENSUS COMMUNIS'

The spectator is always one of many. We share a response to spectacle
with other audience members. By noticing what is held in common in
our different responses to the spectacle, we become aware that we
share a common way of experiencing the world – a 'common sense', or
'Sensus Communis' as Kant calls it. This is an altogether different thing
from what we usually mean by common sense. It is not a faculty for
seeing the obvious, but a sense for the good and the beautiful that is held
in common between the different spectators, however they may differ on
their particular interpretations of the play. It is this 'Sensus Communis',
this shared human way of experiencing the world that, according to
Arendt, had become lost through the experience of totalitarianism.

BEAUTY AND SINGULARITY

Let us think a bit more about how Kant's theory of judgement helped
Arendt to form her unique perspective on the trial of Adolf
Eichmann. Kant's concern is with the singularity of the beautiful.
Beauty is only ever found in particular examples of the beautiful,
rather than in an abstract, theoretical idea of what beauty is. Kant
argues that we act as if an idea of the beautiful existed, that we 'talk
about the beautiful as if beauty were a characteristic of the object and
the judgement were logical' (Kant 1987: 54), but in reality there are
only particular experiences of beauty.

This awareness that there is no absolute rule for the beautiful has
been hugely enabling for modernist literary writing in English. The
American modernist writer Gertrude Stein (1874–1946) wrote that 'rose
is a rose is a rose'. The rose has been a symbol of natural beauty for hun-
dreds of years, but in Stein's poem it is no longer a symbol at all. The rose
is no longer a beautiful thing that can be made to stand for something else –
to represent, for example, the idea of love, or of Englishness, or of innocence. In Stein's poem, the rose is a particular thing that only ever leads
back to itself, that cannot be generalised into the status of a symbol.

REFLECTIVE VERSUS DETERMINANT
JUDGEMENT

Following Kant, Arendt defines the way in which we judge the beautiful
as 'reflective judgement', and contrasts it with the kind of judgement

that goes on in a court of law and that Kant calls 'determinant judgement':

> Determinant judgments subsume the particular under a general rule; reflective judgements, on the contrary, 'derive' the rule from the particular.
>
> (LKPP: 83)

Whereas reflective judgements are judgements of particular beautiful objects that lack a guiding idea of the beautiful, determinant judgements have a rule to guide them. When a judgement is made in a court of law, for example, the law determines for the judge what is legal and illegal, and the task of the judge is simply to apply the law to the particular case in hand. Arendt thought that it was precisely this having of legal and moral rules, and with it the possibility of making determinant judgements, that had been destroyed by the experience of totalitarian rule. In her epilogue to *Eichmann in Jerusalem*, she writes of how under totalitarian rule,

> there were no rules to be abided by, under which the particular cases with which [individuals] were confronted could be subsumed. They had to decide each instance as it arose, because no rules existed for the unprecedented.
>
> (EJ: 295).

Arendt suggests that the totalitarian environment of Nazi Germany placed individuals in a situation that called for reflective judgement. The individual in a totalitarian environment was confronted with an increasingly bizarre and unexpected series of events, and was forced to make judgements about each event 'as it arose'. No 'set of rules' could be used as a guide for the completely unexpected events that unfolded in Nazi Germany. Arendt claims that the majority of the population had failed to face up to the challenge of this new reality; rather than finding a new way to judge it, she argues that their consciences had simply collapsed. Eichmann, to this extent, is typical of what human beings are capable of if the political state undermines the community's shared set of public moral and legal values. Arendt thought that, depressingly enough, in such a situation most individuals do not fight for those values, but rather conform to the new, bizarre and unpredictable social reality.

Arendt thought that the court in Jerusalem, like the people of Nazi Germany, needed to make a reflective judgement, and that it too had failed to meet this challenging new reality. Any attempt to determine Eichmann's actions according to established legal and moral standards risked blunting the court's perception of the radical change in human nature that Eichmann embodied. Arendt thought that, unfortunately, the court had failed to live up to this demand. Confronted with authentic perplexities at Eichmann's behaviour, the court resorted to making Eichmann's case symbolise all of the unresolved questions that had emerged from the Holocaust, such as '"How could it happen?" and "Why did it happen?" or "Why the Jews?" and "Why the Germans?"' (EJ: 5). According to Arendt, this did not serve the cause of justice. She argued that the danger with conflating Eichmann's story with the whole narrative of the Nazi genocide and with the whole history of anti-Semitism was that, paradoxically, it risked exonerating Eichmann from his crimes:

> If the defendant is taken as a symbol and the trial as a pretext to bring up matters which are apparently more interesting than the guilt or innocence of one person, then consistency demands that we bow to the assertion made by Eichmann and his lawyer: that he was brought to book because a scapegoat was needed [...] for anti-Semitism and totalitarian government as well as for the human race and original sin.
>
> (EJ: 286)

The court in Jerusalem had failed to apply itself to the strange particularity of Eichmann, and had instead made him into a symbol of the whole criminal enterprise of Nazi Germany, and even the whole history of human wrongdoing. Arendt is not suggesting that the court in Jerusalem had offered a 'show trial', but that in failing to face the singularity and newness of Eichmann's crimes, it had missed an historic opportunity to understand what happened to the human personality under totalitarianism.

EICHMANN'S STORY

In her book, Arendt sought to make the reflective judgement of Eichmann that the court had failed to make. In order to do this, she needed to imagine a new idea of justice that fitted the new, post-totalitarian conditions of the post-war world. This idea and practice of justice proceeded by telling the story of Eichmann's life. The act of storytelling sought to isolate what was particular about Eichmann and his story from the much bigger issues that the trial in Jerusalem had wanted to hang onto his story. Arendt did not assume that Eichmann was lying, and trying to hide his real malevolence. Rather, she assumed that Eichmann, like any other actor appearing in public space, could not but disclose his real identity to the court. Arendt took Eichmann's story as symptomatic of the bewildering break in human history and tradition that totalitarianism had effected. Like the judgement of the court, then, Arendt's judgement of Eichmann in her story implied that general conclusions could be drawn from this particular case. But unlike the judgement of the court, Arendt's judgement sought out these general conclusions from the life-story itself. To this extent, it might be defined as the reflective judgement that was missing from the official Israeli verdict.

Who, then, was Eichmann, according to Hannah Arendt? Far from thinking of him as a monster, Arendt concluded that Eichmann was 'terrifyingly normal' (EJ: 276). Eichmann's values were solidly bourgeois. 'What he fervently believed in', Arendt writes, 'was success, the chief standard of "good society"' (EJ: 126). The trial had shown how the most 'normal' member of society, when he finds that the fabric of social reality is starting to fray, or when he feels the solid ground of the world shifting beneath his feet, is capable of involving himself in the most appalling of crimes, if he thinks (wrongly, as it turned out) that this involvement will allow him to hang on to his place in the respectable, bourgeois world.

Eichmann displayed a typical bourgeois morality in his insistence to the court that he had never acted from what he described as 'base motives' (EJ: 25). Rather than assuming that this was a smokescreen that Eichmann had put up in order to hide his real monstrosity, Arendt, again, took him at his word. But how could someone who claims to have never acted in a base way have ended up involved in the Final Solution? Why was it that Eichmann's conscience seemed not to work during the Second World War? Why was it that he could let his professional ambition overrule his awareness of the absolute criminality of what he was involved in?

Eichmann was essentially a bureaucrat, responsible for organising the transportations of Jews from the German Reich to the death and labour camps in the east. Although he was not involved in the killing, there can be no question that Eichmann knew exactly the fate that awaited those he was responsible for transporting to the concentration camps. Eichmann had made numerous trips to Auschwitz, and been sent to Minsk in Russia in 1941 to report on the mass killing of Jews by shooting (he told his commander, Heinrich Muller, that he was 'not "tough enough" for what he had seen' (EJ: 89)), and he was fully apprised of the plan to exterminate all the Jews in German-occupied territories not long after it was taken. Yet none of this stopped Eichmann, with his normal and average bourgeois morality, from carrying out his job with meticulous thoroughness. How could this be so? Arendt thought that important answers to these questions too were revealed in Eichmann's appearance before the court and, in particular, through Eichmann's use of language. Arendt noted a horrible banality in Eichmann's speech, and she observed in particular that he 'was genuinely incapable of uttering a single sentence that was not a cliché' (EJ: 48). She took this lack of originality in Eichmann's way of expressing himself to be symptomatic of a much deeper problem in his personality:

> The longer one listened to him, the more obvious it became that his inability to speak was closely connected with an inability to think, namely, to think from the standpoint of somebody else. No communication was possible with him, not because he lied but because he was surrounded by the most reliable of safeguards against the words and the presence of others, and hence against reality as such.
>
> (EJ: 49)

Eichmann had surrounded himself with a defensive shield in the banality of his language, a way of expressing himself which absolved him from the need to think and communicate with others. Paradoxically, this inability to think with a Kantian 'enlarged mentality', an inability to think 'from the standpoint of somebody else', meant that Eichmann took the cue for his behaviour from the actions of everyone around him. Arendt writes that 'the most potent fact in the soothing of his own conscience was the simple fact that he could see no one, no one at all, who actually was against the Final Solution' (EJ: 116). The story of Eichmann shows that the conformist, bourgeois personality is more than willing and able to conform to standards of absolute criminality if he sees everyone around him doing the same.

CONCLUSIONS

What general conclusions can be drawn from the particular story of Adolf Eichmann? Perhaps he can teach us about the reasons why the German middle class supported Hitler's rise to power. They did so, judging by the example of Eichmann, because Hitler promised to allow them to remain bourgeois in a world in which their class position seemed to be threatened. But more than anything, according to Arendt, the bourgeois man refused to take a stand against Hitler simply because he could see no one around him taking such a stand. The phenomenon of mass conformism kept Hitler in power.

The other topic of this chapter has been the status of justice in a post-totalitarian, post-metaphysical world. We have seen how Kant's *Critique of Judgement*, and in particular his theory of reflective judgement, offered Arendt crucial resources for thinking about the problem of how to make meaningful judgements in a world where all absolute standards have collapsed. Arendt's use of Kant in this way mirrors his importance for other critical thinkers who have been preoccupied with issues of justice and singularity, such as the postmodern philosopher Jean-François Lyotard (1924–98). As we will see in the chapters that follow, the question of what justice means is a real and political, rather than an abstract philosophical issue for our age. Arendt's work on Eichmann blazes a trial for what is a crucial issue in political and philosophical modernity.

6

ANTI-SEMITISM

This chapter will begin to look at Arendt's monumental work *The Origins of Totalitarianism* (1951). Arendt had worked on the book throughout the war years, and completed it in the late 1940s in America, as more and more information about the full horror of the totalitarian regimes in Russia and Germany was emerging. The book is divided into three separate volumes: 'Anti-Semitism', 'Imperialism' and 'Totalitarianism', and these will be considered each in turn in this chapter and the two that follow. The first two volumes of the book seek to understand and to explain the formation of certain 'elements' that appeared in European society, roughly in the sixty years from 1870 to 1930, and that later 'crystallised' into the totalitarian movements of Hitler's Nazism and Stalin's communism. The three most important of these elements were modern anti-Semitism, imperialism, and the collapse of the nation-state. This chapter will deal exclusively with the first of these, which presents a complex and fascinating subject for Arendt's historical understanding. We will look at Arendt's use of literary writings by modern Jewish writers, in particular Marcel Proust (1871–1922) and Franz Kafka (1883–1924), to think about the paradoxes of modern anti-Semitism.

TOTALITARIANISM AND HISTORY

Throughout her life's work, Arendt remained committed to the view that totalitarianism was an entirely new and unprecedented event in the history of human society, and that as such it called for a new model of historical understanding in order to make sense of it. The trial of Adolf Eichmann in 1961 showed, according to Arendt, that traditional ideas of justice, criminality and personal responsibility were incapable of accounting for the thoroughly new and disturbing nature of the crimes committed by the totalitarian regimes (see Chapter 5). In a similar way, in *The Origins of Totalitarianism*, Arendt questioned the ability of established frameworks for historical understanding to make sense of the totalitarian movements, their origins and their organisation. The elements of totalitarianism are not then to be understood as 'causes' of totalitarianism, as they might be in a more conventional historical narrative. Instead, Arendt turned to story-telling, as she was to do again ten years later in the case of Eichmann, in order to formulate a new method of historical understanding that made sense of these new and almost incomprehensible events.

Arendt argues that the elements of totalitarianism found in late nineteenth- and early twentieth-century society did not 'cause' totalitarianism as such because they did not lead inevitably to it. Things might always have turned out otherwise. At the same time, Arendt's book assumes that certain new kinds of experience that entered into European social and political life in the late nineteenth century and the early twentieth century did have a formative influence on the totalitarian movements. This period saw the invention of new forms of social experience and new types of human personality that became central to the criminal practices of totalitarianism. For example, Arendt argues that the kind of personality that could become involved in the genocide against the Jews in Europe was actually invented in the brutalising imperialist adventures of the European powers in Africa (see Chapter 7). Similarly, her book claims that the complex psychology of Nazi anti-Semitism was invented in European society in the late nineteenth century.

STORYTELLING AND TOTALITARIANISM

From the perspective of conventional historical understanding, which focuses on verifiable links between different historical events, such claims as Arendt's might seem to be tenuous to say the least. But Arendt found that the relationship between totalitarianism and its elements could be captured in a much more authentic and meaningful way by telling the story of totalitarianism, rather than by trying to write its history. In 1958, Arendt described how, when she first wrote her book, her intentions presented themselves to her 'in the form of an ever recurring image: I felt as though I dealt with a crystallized structure which I had to break up into its constituent elements in order to destroy it' (cited in Kohn 2002: 626). There is, then, a destructive element to Arendt's storytelling in *The Origins of Totalitarianism*. She seeks literally to break down the 'crystallised structure' of totalitarianism into its constituent parts. By telling the story of totalitarianism, in other words, Arendt wants to deconstruct totalitarianism itself. Her book does not aim only to understand totalitarianism in a static, intellectual way, but to actively oppose it and resist it, and ultimately to contribute to its destruction. In working backwards from the structure to its elements, Arendt also aims to preserve an understanding of how these 'elements' did not lead inevitably to totalitarianism. Rather, it was the particular combination of the elements, and the social conditions that made this combination possible, that opened up the space in European society for totalitarianism.

THINKING ABOUT ANTI-SEMITISM

In telling the story of modern anti-Semitism, Arendt engages with a question that had puzzled social theorists and critical thinkers for over a century before the publication of her book. For many of those thinkers, such as Karl Marx, the question of fraught social relations between Jews and Gentiles offered a useful way of thinking about some of the inherent contradictions in bourgeois society. Anti-Semitism had remained an important issue in the Marxist tradition, and the final chapter of the Marxist critical theorists Max Horkheimer and Theodor Adorno's book *Dialectic of Enlightenment* (1944) had been devoted to it. More recently, the deconstructionist Jacques Derrida and the postmodernist Jean-François Lyotard have both written extensively about anti-Semitism as a philosophical, historical and textual problem.

While Arendt agrees with these other thinkers that anti-Semitism has been a defining problem for modern society, her particular interest is in tracing the winding path that took anti-Semitism from nineteenth-century European society into Nazi propaganda and ideology. This involved Arendt in an inquiry into the complex self-consciousness that Jews developed in a non-Jewish society that, paradoxically, seemed to be perpetually in the act of both including and excluding them from itself. Arendt's study of anti-Semitism requires some understanding of the political and social history of the Jews in Europe, and this chapter will begin by considering these different issues. At the end of the chapter, we will also look at some of Arendt's fascinating and disturbing insights into the psychology of anti-Semitism.

ANTI-SEMITISM AND POLITICS

Arendt's telling of the story of the origins of totalitarianism takes her to the drawing rooms of European high society at the end of the nineteenth century. She asks why it was that anti-Semitism, which eventually became central to Nazi ideology, was so prominent in the social life of Europe at this time. Arendt proposes a unique form of philosophical–social history that looks at how a new, distinctively modern form of anti-Semitism could prepare the way for the genocide committed by the Nazis. As the Arendt critic George Kateb usefully reminds us, however, 'Antisemitism need not have led to extermination camps; but they would not have existed had not European peoples made antisemitism a regular part of their way of looking at the world' (Kateb 1984: 58). Arendt's study offers an at times controversial attempt to get inside the social experience of late nineteenth-century Europe, and thereby to recover a sense of what it felt like to be anti-Semitic, or to be the victim of anti-Semitism. As Kateb writes:

> [Arendt] is painstaking in her effort to make modern antisemitism in Europe an intelligible social and political tendency. The method of intelligibility is the attempt to think the thoughts of antisemites, to study and half imagine the ways in which they saw and felt the world.
>
> (Kateb 1984: 61)

Arendt's book proposes a unique method of social history. She uses her power of imagination to identify the thoughts and feelings of historical actors, Jews and anti-Semites alike, and to reconstruct their ways of seeing the world and their experiences. As we will see, this method led her towards some very unexpected and occasionally disturbing insights.

THE 'JEWISH QUESTION'

Arendt's book seeks to recover a political understanding of modern anti-Semitism. She writes that it has been 'one of the most unfortunate facts in the history of the Jewish people that only its enemies, and almost never its friends, understood that the Jewish question was a political one' (OT1: 56). What was the 'Jewish question'? In his book *Hannah Arendt and the Jewish Question*, Richard Bernstein writes that the term 'was used to designate a whole series of shifting, loosely related, historical, cultural, religious, economic, political, and social issues' (Bernstein 1996: xi). The Jewish question indicated a complicated set of overlapping issues that we need to think about before looking in more detail at Arendt's book.

Throughout the nineteenth century, there had been numerous attempts made to answer the so-called Jewish question by prominent thinkers and journalists, such as Karl Marx in his essay 'On the Jewish Question' (1843) and the leading Zionist, Theodor Herzl (1860–1904) in his pamphlet *The Jewish State* (1896). Jews had been granted political freedom, or emancipation as it is more commonly called, in many European states in the first decades of the nineteenth century. The principles of the Enlightenment and the French Revolution had tried to separate religion from politics, and to make religion a matter of conscience, and as such a strictly non-political issue. Being a Jew, or a Catholic, or a Protestant consequently became a private matter, officially at least in the eyes of many states, and so Jews were made, in constitutional terms, equal with other members of society. But this new political freedom was not replicated in civil society, where Jews were not yet fully integrated, or assimilated in the more common term, into the non-Jewish community, and where they continued to suffer from anti-Semitism, despite their new-found political freedom. The Jewish question then sought to resolve the ongoing social problem of relations between Jews and their neighbours. For a Zionist such as Herzl, the question could be resolved only by granting the Jews their own state; for a communist like Marx, the Jewish question, like all other social problems, would be solved only by getting rid of the state altogether.

Modern anti-Semitism is different from earlier forms of anti-Semitism because it springs from the tensions that arose between Jews and Gentiles as they lived alongside one another in society, with common civil liberties, rather than in separate communities. For Marx, the fact that political emancipation had not solved the Jewish question pointed towards a wider tension between politics and society. Marx argued that even after the granting of political freedoms, a pervasive sense of coercion continued to be felt within the private spaces of civil society, and that therefore politics in their current, bourgeois form could not solve social problems. Marx argued in his essay 'On the Jewish Question' that this conflict between political freedom and social coercion meant that man leads a 'double life' in bourgeois society:

> In the *political community* he regards himself as a *communal being*; but in *civil society* he is active as a *private individual*, treats other men as means, reduces himself to a means, and becomes the plaything of alien powers.
>
> (Marx 1997: 225)

Marx claimed that this divided existence was a problem for all members of society, and not just for Jews. Arendt's work on anti-Semitism built on Marx's awareness of bourgeois society as an unfree space, although she thought that anti-Semitism had developed a particular and unique status of its own as a social problem. But the intervening history of totalitarianism between Marx's and Arendt's analyses of the Jewish question had made it much more difficult for Arendt to recover a political response to the Jewish question than it had been for Marx. Given that the Nazis had eventually proposed a 'Final Solution' to this Jewish question, in the mass extermination of the Jewish people, the seriousness of the original question had been somewhat forgotten, and even posing the question had come to seem tainted with anti-Semitism. Nevertheless, this is just what Arendt seeks to do.

ANTI-SEMITISM AND SOCIETY

Arendt claims that, with political emancipation and partial assimilation into non-Jewish society, Jews began to develop a social identity of their own, as they were no longer defined solely as a religious group, or conversely in terms of the economic power of the large, international

Jewish banking families of Europe such as the Rothschilds. Assimilated Jews might now appear in society as artists, philosophers or (very occasionally) as politicians. However, Arendt argues that the social identity of Jews that emerged from this new-found freedom was shaped much more out of the failures of assimilation than from any new-found social acceptability:

> Society, confronted with political, economic and legal equality for Jews, made it quite clear that none of its classes was prepared to grant them social equality, and that only exceptions from the Jewish people would be received.
>
> (OT1: 56)

Arendt claims that the general Jewish population was not granted acceptance into society, but that particular Jews who seemed to stand out from the mass of their brethren were admitted. Arendt examines the new Jewish social identity of these 'exception Jews', or 'parvenus' as she calls them, borrowing a term from the French Jewish journalist Bernard Lazare (1865–1903). *Parvenu* is a French term that, in both French and English signifies the social type of the newly wealthy member of the bourgeoisie, the 'new money' that emerged with the development of industry and commerce in the nineteenth century. Arendt understands this figure of the wealthy, successful Jew, newly arrived in society and desperate to fit in and to escape his obscure origins, as a key personality type in the formation of totalitarian anti-Semitism. She argues that the terms on which these 'exception' Jews were admitted into high society in the late nineteenth century were highly questionable. In particular, she argues that at this period, '[t]he Enlightenment's genuine tolerance and curiosity for everything human was being replaced by a morbid lust for the exotic, abnormal and different as such' (OT1: 68).

THE JEWS AND THE ENLIGHTENMENT

Arendt thought that the culture of the Enlightenment of the eighteenth century had shown a rational interest and tolerance for those who are racially and culturally different, and had sought to emphasise the idea of their common humanity. The key figure for Arendt in this Enlightenment discourse of tolerance was the German writer and philosopher G.E. Lessing (1729–81). In an essay from 1932 called

'The Enlightenment and the Jewish Question', Arendt describes Lessing's idea that 'deep inside every human being – despite differences of dogmatic convictions, morals, and conduct – is the same human being' (JW: 3). However, Arendt claims that, by the end of the nineteenth century, European societies had given up on these Enlightenment principles, and that Parisian high society of the 1890s in particular had become bored with the morality of the Enlightenment, which it thought to be bourgeois and hypocritical. Society still retained its interest in cultural and racial others, but this had, according to Arendt, degenerated from enlightened tolerance into an unhealthy and morbid 'lust for the exotic'. Instead of seeking out a common humanity in those who are racially different, the new society became interested in exoticising and fetishising their difference. It wanted, according to Arendt, to indulge in a taste for 'difference as such'.

PARVENU VERSUS PARIAH

Opposed against the figure of the Jewish parvenu who wants to fit in, Arendt pitches another character type borrowed from Lazare, the 'pariah'. Pariah is a word of Sanskrit origin, indicating those who were at the bottom of India's caste system or even outside it – 'outcastes'. Lazare, and after him Arendt, use it to indicate those Jews (the majority of them, in fact) who remained beyond the pale of civil society. A key point about the pariah, for Arendt, is that he cannot be politically active, since he exists outside society. Both Lazare and Arendt seek to politicise the category of the pariah, and to claim that the pariahs were a kind of revolutionary Jewish political power in waiting. Lazare argued that being a pariah, a social outsider, could seem like quite an attractive option to certain wealthy and educated Jews, since it allowed the person who recognised himself as a pariah to fashion an identity as a kind of romantic outsider. But to do so, he thought, would be to shirk the political responsibility of the pariah. Lazare identified a further subcategory of the pariah, the 'conscious pariah'. In an essay which she wrote in 1944, 'The Jew as Pariah: A Hidden Tradition', Arendt describes Lazare's understanding of the 'conscious pariah':

> [I]n contrast to his unemancipated brethren who accept their pariah status automatically and unconsciously, the emancipated Jew must awake to an awareness of his position and, conscious of it, become a rebel against it – the

champion of an oppressed people. His fight for freedom is part and parcel of
that which all the downtrodden of Europe must wage to achieve national and
social liberation.

(JW: 283)

The conscious pariah has refused to become a parvenu. He refuses to
ingratiate himself into non-Jewish society, to become a parvenu, but
he equally refuses to revel in a romantic ideal of his status as an outsider, or to passively accept that status. Rather, he actively recognises and
struggles against that status. Paradoxically, Arendt argues in her essay,
once this outsider figure affirms and rebels against his outsider status,
he will become a key representative of a more general human condition of being excluded and 'downtrodden'. 'As soon as the pariah
enters the arena of politics and translates his status into political
terms,' writes Arendt, 'he becomes perforce a rebel' (JW: 284). One
of the great paradoxes of the failures of Jewish emancipation and
assimilation, as Lazare understood it (and Arendt after him), was that
in becoming conscious of his outsider status, and in making it public,
the Jewish pariah could become a representative rebel, and blaze a
trail for other oppressed or excluded peoples.

KAFKA

In her essay, Arendt looks for examples of the conscious pariah among
Jewish artists. She poses a brilliant reading of Franz Kafka's novel *The
Castle* (1926) as an allegory of the failures of assimilation, and of the
political potential of the self-conscious pariah. Kafka, who is now
thought to have been one of the finest novelists of the twentieth century,
was practically unknown when Arendt was writing about him; she and
Walter Benjamin were two of his earliest advocates. Kafka's is a disturbing, surreal and uncanny novel about the struggle of a protagonist,
known only as K (and who for Arendt is 'plainly Jewish'). K wants to
start making a life for himself in an unfamiliar village which is at the
foot of a castle with which he is in some undefined way associated.
The paradox of Kafka's novel is that all that K wants is to be treated
normally, to become indistinguishable from the villagers by working
and having a family, but the harder he tries to achieve this, the more
strange he seems to them. In particular, he cannot escape the association with the castle that he holds for the villagers. Arendt argues

that K's desire for assimilation – for a life in which he is no longer constantly an exception – becomes revolutionary. Arendt writes of K's developing relationship with the villagers that 'His story, his behaviour, has taught them both that human rights are worth fighting for and that the rule of the castle is not divine law and, consequently, can be attacked' (JW: 295). *The Castle*, according to Arendt, tells the story of how, in coming to a realisation about the failure of his efforts to assimilate into non-Jewish society, the Jew can make others aware of how the development of their own freedom is obstructed. The self-conscious pariah becomes an archetypal political rebel.

If we compare this treatment of the paradoxes of assimilation to Marx's in 'The Jewish Question', and look at it in the light of Lazare's politicisation of the category of the pariah, it becomes clear that Arendt's reading of Kafka poses a way of moving from the Jewish individual's experience of the problems of assimilation to the general question of social injustice. Unlike Marx, Arendt does not simply bracket the problem of anti-Semitism as a kind of symptom of the injustices inherent in the general social formation. Rather, Kafka, in Arendt's reading of him, is attentive to how what is specific about Jewish experience takes its place in those wider social paradoxes and restraints, and to the way in which the Jew can act within them. Once again, storytelling proposes a more attentive engagement with experience than theory.

Writing her essay in 1944, Arendt understood the categories of pariah and parvenu to have been exploded by the new totalitarian realities. She writes that 'the bottom has dropped out of the old ideology. The pariah Jew and the parvenu Jew are in the same boat, rowing desperately in the same angry sea' (JW: 296). The parvenu's desire to fit in, and the conscious pariah's understanding of himself as an outsider, had become equally meaningless in the light of totalitarian anti-Semitism. As Arendt writes at the end of 'The Jew as Pariah', 'Both the realism of the one and the idealism of the other are today utopian' (JW: 296). Arendt thought, however, that understanding the current catastrophe required a recovery of the categories of pariah and parvenu, and the development of a critical understanding of them. In order to achieve this, in *The Origins of Totalitarianism* she examines the status of the parvenu in Paris in the late nineteenth century, when the modern, totalitarian form of anti-Semitism was first invented.

According to Arendt, Paris led the way among European societies in the new fascination with exotic difference that characterised pre-totalitarian societies. Arendt claims that Paris, which, in the words of Walter Benjamin, had been 'the capital of the nineteenth century', was by the end of that century 'left without political significance and social splendor, to the intellectual avant-garde of all countries' (OT1: 79). It is in the work of the artists and intellectuals who flocked to Paris that the social life of the 1890s, and the modern form of anti-Semitism that, according to Arendt, took root there, finds its most vivid record. Arendt argues that this new form of anti-Semitism became a crucial element in the totalitarianism of the Nazi state.

PROUST

In *The Origins of Totalitarianism*, Arendt takes literary narrative, in particular the novel, to offer a crucial source of knowledge about the new status of Jews in European society. She describes how

> [s]ocial factors, unaccounted for in political or economic history, hidden under the surface of events, [are] never perceived by the historian and recorded only by the more penetrating and passionate force of poets and novelists.
>
> (OT1: 87)

There are certain aspects of social existence, Arendt argues, that remain invisible to the gaze of the historian with his preoccupation with economic and political facts, and that appear instead in the work of novelists. In thinking about the role played by anti-Semitism in Paris society in the 1890s, Arendt turns to the work of the French novelist Marcel Proust, the author of a key novel in literary modernism, *Remembrance of Things Past* (1913–27). Proust is an ideal source for Arendt's effort to reconstruct the place of Jews in French social experience, both because he spent his life 'exclusively in society' (OT1: 80) and because he was half-Jewish. According to Arendt, Proust's work contributes to a social history of the Jews in France at a time when their identity was undergoing a rapid transformation.

JEWISHNESS AS A CRIME/VICE

In its lust for the exotic, Parisian high society developed a new type of fascination with Jews, and one that was much more disturbing and unstable than the rational, tolerant fascination with them that Arendt finds in the culture of the Enlightenment. She argues that Proust's writing provides evidence for how Jews reacted to and adapted to this new fascination with their difference, and how in many cases the parvenu Jews played along with the idea of their exotic abnormality. The fact that these exception Jews found themselves in this situation was an unintended consequence of their political emancipation, which had made of their Jewishness a private matter:

> The result was that their private lives, their decisions and sentiments, became the very center of their "Jewishness". And the more the fact of Jewish birth lost its religious, national, and socio-economic significance, the more obsessive Jewishness became; Jews were obsessed by it as one may be by a physical defect or advantage, and addicted to it as one may be to a vice.
>
> (OT1: 84)

This passage gives a good sense of how uncomfortable Arendt's writing can be in its attempt to get inside the disturbing social space of late nineteenth-century Paris. Arendt argues that it took only a short step to move from understanding Jewishness as a private matter to understanding it as something hidden, like a physical defect or a vice. Arendt further argues that once Jewishness had become a private matter, and an 'obsession' among Jews themselves, it took only another small step for Jewishness to be thought of, in Proust's terms, as an 'innate predisposition'. Jewishness became an inherent, racial condition, and at the same time, an old stereotype was recycled in the modern social environment: Jews are innately predisposed to commit crimes. It was this complex sense of Jewishness as something that is innate, a racial characteristic, and also as something inward, something that might be hidden from others and that is bound up with criminality, that found its way into Nazi ideology.

It must be said that Arendt is very unclear about how the anti-Semitism of Parisian high society in the 1890s morphed into Nazi anti-Semitism. As we will see in the next chapter, Arendt is often able to be quite specific and concrete about how imperialist ideologies and practices found their way into the totalitarian movements. But it is fair to say that Arendt herself remained fairly perplexed about how 'the Jewish question and antisemitism, relatively unimportant phenomena in terms of world politics, became the catalytic agent for [...] the rise of the Nazi movement' (OT1: x). A catalytic agent, in

Arendt's analogy between history and chemistry, is not a part of the thing that is produced or 'crystallised' through the catalysis; but at the same time that thing clearly could not have existed without it. The only twentieth-century political movement that Arendt thought was directly caused by nineteenth-century anti-Semitism was not Nazism but Zionism (OT1: xi). Perhaps the best way to understand anti-Semitism's relation to Nazism, then, would be to say that the former created the ideological conditions of possibility for the latter.

Arendt describes how in Parisian high society in the 1890s a complex game was played, whereby particular Jews who were accepted into society pretended to hide their Jewishness as if it were a vice. The open secret of this vice was titillating, argues Arendt, for a society that wanted to be thrilled by its association with all manner of people who represented an escape from bourgeois morality, such as criminals and artists. Proust was gay, and Arendt persistently claims that Jewishness and homosexuality, along with crime, became equivalent indulgences for a society on the lookout for 'perversion':

> In both cases, society was far from being prompted by a revision of prejudices. They did not doubt that homosexuals were "criminals" or that Jews were "traitors"; they only revised their attitude toward crime and treason […] The best-hidden disease of the nineteenth century, its terrible boredom and general weariness, had burst like an abscess.
>
> (OT1: 81)

An indulgence with the thrilling danger of crime or vice was only destined to be short-lived. Arendt writes that 'in a moment it can switch to a decision to liquidate not only all actual criminals but all who are "racially" predestined to commit certain crimes' (OT1: 81). Arendt's book gestures towards the path taken by anti-Semitism in the twentieth century. Starting out as a desire on the part of a bored society to smash the phoney morality of the Enlightenment through an association with Jews who were thought to be treacherous and deceitful, anti-Semitism turned into a collective decision to purge society of that attraction to vice, and to liquidate those who had been defined as treacherous and criminal. The burst abscess of the high bourgeois society of the late nineteenth century was to be cleansed by the totalitarian policy of liquidating the criminals and traitors (gay people were also victims of the Nazi genocide). Arendt notes a complex psychology determining modern anti-Semitism, which involves a mingled attraction and repulsion towards Jews. She claims that the attraction and repulsion were often found in the same individual, often at the same time, and this insight leads her to some rather disturbing conclusions. She asks, for example, why it was that 'these "admirers" of Jews finally became their murderers' (OT1: 86).

Arendt's analysis of Proust and anti-Semitism highlights a central paradox in Jewish assimilation: just at the moment when Jews became politically free, no longer singled out or distinguished by the state, an inward, psychological idea of Jewish difference and alterity became a crucial feature of social life. Jews, argues Arendt, were asked to 'play the role society had assigned them' (OT1: 86). Society defined them as untrustworthy and treacherous – which was essentially no different from how they had been defined since medieval times – but what had changed was that Jews now took that role on themselves, and pretended to be secretive and treacherous when, in fact, they had nothing to hide. The kind of social behaviour that Arendt describes here has more recently been defined as 'peer pressure'. In other words, Jews performed a version of themselves that society expected of them – they played up to certain stereotypes about Jewishness that society wanted to see confirmed. This was, for Jews, a very unstable situation in which to find themselves, and liable to collapse at any point.

CASE STUDY 7: ARENDT AND FANON

Arendt's willingness to reimagine the psychology and standpoint of the anti-Semite can certainly make the contemporary reader feel uncomfortable. In particular, it can seem unsympathetic to the victims of anti-Semitism, both in the way that it entertains with some seriousness the world view of their oppressors, and in the way that it highlights the collusion of some Jews with the formation of the oppressive stereotype. But examined from another point of view, Arendt offers a perceptive and prescient account of the question of Jewish social and cultural identity. Her work on anti-Semitism compares in this regard with that of her contemporary, the psychiatrist, critic of colonialism and political revolutionary Frantz Fanon (1925–61) who analysed the subjectivity foisted on black people in a dominantly white society. Although in a later essay, *On Violence* (1970), Arendt criticises Fanon for making violence the basis of his political activism in his book

The Wretched of the Earth (1961), there is some consonance between their earlier writings, and in particular their shared advocacy of political activism. Like Arendt, Fanon used the dominant philosophical currents of the day, existentialism and phenomenology, in order to think about the experience of racism. In *Black Skin/White Masks*, which was published in French in the same year as *The Origins of Totalitarianism*, 1951, Fanon shows how the black man cannot act in a spontaneous way in a white-dominated society. Fanon engages in a complex psychological self-analysis, and describes how he, as a black man, experiences his own identity through a set of stereotypes, prejudices and anecdotes that in fact belong to white society.

> I was responsible at the same time for my body, for my race, for my ancestors. I subjected myself to an objective examination, I discovered my blackness, my ethnic characteristics; and I was battered down by tom-toms, cannibalism, intellectual deficiency, fetishism, racial defects, slave-ships, and above all else, above all: 'Sho' good eatin'.
>
> (Fanon 1991: 112)

In his awareness of how his identity is conditioned by a set of presuppositions and anecdotes, and in his awareness of how he is forced to carry a whole history of blackness in expressing his identity, Fanon's work on blackness compares interestingly with Arendt's on anti-Semitism. Both point towards ways in which the Jewish/black other internalises the stereotype held by white society about them, and how this internalisation leads him to perpetuate that stereotype. Through her idea of the conscious pariah, and through Fanon's advocacy of violent revolution, both also propose forms of activism that seek to recover the ability of the marginalised self to define his or her own identity.

CONCLUSION

This chapter has examined the first volume of Arendt's study, *The Origins of Totalitarianism*. It has traced Arendt's argument that a new and distinctively modern and social form of anti-Semitism was born out of the failures of the emancipation of the Jews in nineteenth-century European society. It has shown how Arendt poses this argument in the form of a story, and also shown how she drew upon the work of novelists, such as Proust and Kafka, in order to recover vital evidence about the evolution of this new form of anti-Semitism. We have looked at the missed opportunity for a new form of Jewish political activism proposed by the figure of the 'conscious pariah'. Finally, we looked at Arendt's claim that some Jews played up to the social stereotypes that were formed about them in this period, and at how this left them in a very precarious social position.

7

RACISM, EMPIRE AND NATION

The second volume of *The Origins of Totalitarianism* shows an early and highly perceptive interest in a number of topics that have more recently become the concern of postcolonial studies, such as race, ethnicity, nationality and empire. The intersection between Arendt's work and postcolonial literary and cultural studies is increasingly being acknowledged by postcolonial critics. In 1994, the editors of *Colonial Discourse and Postcolonial Theory* claimed that the 'insights and methods' of *The Origins of Totalitarianism* 'offer an important source for future colonial discourse theorization' (Williams and Chrisman 1994: 7). Yet while the work of other theorists of race and ethnicity who were contemporary with Arendt, such as Frantz Fanon, have become significant influences on postcolonial studies, Arendt's important work on European imperialism is arguably still under-represented in the field. Undoubtedly, though, her book is an indispensable study for anyone interested in the political significance of the imperial exploitation of Africa, and in particular its literary representations.

In the 'Imperialism' volume of *The Origins of Totalitarianism*, Arendt analyses the ways in which the experience of European imperialism, and in particular the imperial exploitation of Africa by the European powers in the late nineteenth century, formed a crucial element of the later totalitarian regimes, which sought to rule over Europe as an empire. Arendt argues that imperialism contributed to totalitarianism in two decisive ways: by promulgating an entirely new form of racial ideology, and by contributing to the collapse of the system of nation-states in Europe.

IMPERIALIST RACISM

Arendt's analysis of anti-Semitism in the first volume of her book shows it to have been a subtle, nuanced and psychologically complex social phenomenon. When she comes to study European imperialism, an encounter with racial difference is again a crucial factor in her analysis. The racism that she finds in European imperialism is, however, altogether cruder and less psychologically nuanced than the anti-Semitism that went on in European society. Arendt's analysis of racism and imperialism can make the reader feel uncomfortable in the way that it tries to reconstruct the position of the racist, as it had previously sought to imagine the position of the anti-Semite (see Chapter 6). She thinks of the new racial ideology that emerged out of the exploitation of Africa by the European powers as the result of an 'incomprehension' and 'terror' that the imperialists felt in their encounter with native Africans.

> Race was the emergency explanation of human beings whom no European or civilized man could understand and whose humanity so frightened and humiliated the immigrants that they no longer cared to belong to the same human race. Race was the Boers' answer to the overwhelming monstrosity of Africa – a whole continent populated and overpopulated by savages – an explanation of the madness which grasped and illuminated them like "a flash of lightning in a serene sky: 'Exterminate all the brutes'".

(OT2: 65)

A number of Arendt's more recent critics have registered a sense of unease with her effort in passages such as this one to imagine herself into the position of the imperialist or colonialist (Duarte 2007). The tone of such passages almost suggests that Arendt is excusing colonial brutality, and empathising with the 'frightened and humiliated' civilised European in the face of these 'savages'. A brutal response to native peoples was nothing new in European colonialism and imperialism – there had been an ongoing genocide against the native American and Australian aboriginal peoples for over a hundred years, for example, by the time that the exploitation of Africa got fully underway, and slaves had been taken from the West African coast for a similar length of time. But Arendt claims that there were a number of things that were new about the experience of the imperial powers in Africa, as well as in the experience of the Boers, the white Dutch settlers in South Africa, before them. The first of these was the scale of the massacres. Arendt claims that the population of the Congo, which was under Belgian control, had been reduced from between 20 and 40 million to 8 million in the imperial period. Second, what was new about the experience of Africa was that an entirely new racial ideology was established to cope with the 'madness' of these seemingly wild, overpopulated lands. Essentially, this racial ideology suggested that the only way to cope with this problem of over-population was through a policy of genocide. The racial ideology offered a licence to 'exterminate all the brutes'. Third, Arendt claims that what was new about Africa, and what was enabling for the tota-litarian regimes, was that out of the imperialist experience came an entirely new form of political rule.

ARENDT'S RACISM?

In order to make sense of the disturbing tone of Arendt's account of this new form of racism, its apparent sympathy for the racists, it needs to be understood as part of a story, or a work of imaginative identification. Arendt is no more condoning the genocidal response of the imperialists to native Africans than she condones anti-Semitism in Paris in the 1890s. Rather, she is trying to reconstruct the standpoint of the imperialist, because this is the most effective way of recovering the meaning of modern racism, as well as an understanding of how it could have become such an important part of Nazi ideology. The description of Africa as a land of madness and savagery needs to be understood as a literary representation of Africa, an attempt to imagine how Africa must have seemed to the new arrival. In making her argument, Arendt also draws on other literary representations of imperialism in Africa. When Arendt writes 'exterminate all the brutes', for example, she is citing Joseph Conrad's novel *Heart of Darkness* (1902).

My claim about the literariness of her writing does not let Arendt completely off of the hook, however. There is a nonchalance in her use of the word 'savage', as well as in her implicit assumption that the viewpoint of the 'savage' on the brutality that he suffered could not be imagined in her writing (whereas the viewpoint of a genocidal immigrant or Boer, apparently, could). In his book *Culture and Imperialism*, the postcolonial critic Edward Said (1935–2003) understood Conrad as a precursor for Arendt's account of Africa in just these terms:

> Conrad is the precursor of the Western views of the Third World which one finds in the work of novelists as different as Graham Greene, V.S. Naipaul, and Robert Stone, of theoreticians of imperialism like Hannah Arendt […] whose specialty is to deliver the non-European world either for analysis and judgment or for satisfying the exotic tastes of European and North American audiences.
>
> (Said 1993: xix)

Said categorises Arendt's theory alongside the work of novelists who represent the non-European world. He argues that analysis and judgement of the Third World often go hand in hand with exoticising it in the work of fiction writers and theorists. While the question of Arendt's unconscious racism, or Conrad's for that matter, might be debated endlessly, it seems reasonable to assume that literary texts (among which category I include Arendt's writing here) can disclose important dimensions of a racist ideology that they may themselves be implicated in.

THE MOB

In fact, Arendt wrote in very disparaging terms about those who became tools of the new imperialist racial ideology. Arendt writes that 'race, whether as a home-grown ideology in Europe or an emergency explanation for shattering experiences, has always attracted the worst elements in Western civilization' (OT2: 66). This was particularly true in the case of Africa, where the possibility of huge wealth from trading on luxury goods such as gold, diamonds and ivory saw disreputable 'luck hunters' transplant themselves to Africa from Europe, and involve themselves in the brutalisation of native peoples in the pursuit of these commodities.

Arendt argues that these 'luck hunters' mark an important step on the path towards totalitarianism. They were, she says, examples of a new type of social individual who had been produced by the loss of a stable and ordered society in Europe. They were men who had lost a defined and meaningful position in their own society, and for whom imperialism opened up new possibilities of adventure and fortune:

> [T]he luck hunters were not distinctly outside civilized society but, on the contrary, very clearly a by-product of this society, an inevitable residue of the capitalist system and even the representatives of an economy that relentlessly produced a superfluity of men and capital.
>
> (OT2: 69)

Arendt refers to this new type of dislocated humanity as 'the mob', a term which suggests her sense that they were men who had lost a meaningful place in the world, and membership of any organised social body such as a class. The mob is not synonymous for Arendt with the working class, which had a highly defined and organised sense of its social identity and so was, Arendt argues, highly resistant to the seductive rhetoric of the Nazis. The mob was, rather, a residue of all social classes, a kind of mixed up, disorganised body of men who had, in Arendt's terms, become 'rootless'. She understands the mob as a 'by-product' of the capitalistic commodity market, which operates by producing superfluous wealth and waste (see Chapter 4). Arendt argues that imperial adventures overseas enabled European societies to deal temporarily with the problem of this new type of social being, by dumping him onto the rest of the world. She also argues, however, that the new imperial adventurer was to come back to haunt these societies, in the form of what she calls the 'mass man' who later participated in the totalitarian movements (OT3: 13) (see Chapter 8).

IMPERIAL ADVENTURERS: MR KURTZ

Arendt's example of this new type of humanity is Mr Kurtz from Conrad's *Heart of Darkness*, the brutal, amoral commander of an ivory trading post deep in the Belgian Congo:

> Expelled from a world with accepted social values, they had been thrown back upon themselves and still had nothing to fall back upon except, here and there, a streak of talent which made them as dangerous as Kurtz if they were ever allowed to return to their homelands.
>
> (OT2: 69)

Arendt is not suggesting literally that imperial adventurers such as Kurtz returned to Europe and founded the Nazi movement. Rather, her claim is that the new type of human personality that Kurtz represents became a crucial support for the Nazi movement in its early years. This idea is not unique to Arendt, but was first described by the British politician Lord Cromer (1841–1917) as the 'boomerang effect'. Arendt describes Cromer's idea of the 'boomerang effect' very succinctly in her essay *On Violence*: '[R]ule by violence in faraway lands would end by affecting the government of England […] the last "subject race" would be the English themselves' (CR: 153). Arendt claims that such men had learned 'the code of manners which befitted the coming type of murderer' (OT2: 69). Kurtz is described by Conrad as 'hollow to the core' (OT2: 69). He typifies, for Arendt, the member of the mob who has lost his social identity and become violent, self-centred and scheming to the point of insanity in Africa. Arendt claims of the imperial adventurers that 'the only talent that could possibly burgeon in their hollow souls was the gift of fascination which makes a "splendid leader of an extreme party"'. Mr Kurtz wields a charismatic fascination in Conrad's novel; he is first described as 'a very remarkable person' (Conrad 2000: 37). In the time of the action narrated, Kurtz has become a kind of god figure to the natives, whom he rules over with extreme violence. For Arendt, Kurtz foreshadows the type of the charismatic totalitarian leader.

BUREAUCRACY

The second crucial element for totalitarian rule that came out of the imperialist exploitation of Africa is bureaucracy. Arendt argues that during the course of its imperialist adventures in Africa, the British state 'discovered' the idea that bureaucracy could be substituted for a democratically elected government. Arendt argues that the British Empire pioneered an entirely new form of government in Africa, which had not featured in Britain's previous colonial and imperial activity in America, Australia or the Far East. The rule of British territories in Africa was given over to imperial administrators who were unelected. Such a form of government, according to Arendt, was unaccountable to the democratic organs of state, such as parliament in the case of Great Britain. British rule in Africa could therefore escape the authority and criticism of democratic organs of state, and also of public opinion, because of its geographical distance from the centre of that public opinion. The power of bureaucracy also operated by leaving the political status of the new imperialist subjects uncertain. The population that was ruled over in Africa did not have the status of full British citizens, and so they did not enjoy the protection of British law. In other words, the imperialists had discovered that by leaving the political status of the dominated populations of Africa uncertain, it became easy to manipulate and dominate them.

Arendt follows the findings of the sociologist Max Weber, who had examined the ways in which the bureaucratisation and administration of life restrict human freedom, and also the literary writings of Franz Kafka, which examined the same phenomenon in a different way. According to Arendt, the imperialists' idea of making government itself into a form of bureaucracy became a key discovery for the later totalitarian movements. In political terms, what the imperialists had unwittingly discovered was that, if a person or group of people are under the authority of a state but are not full members of that state, there is nothing in the world that can or will stop the state from doing whatever it likes with them. Depressingly, this insight has been proved time and again since the publication of Arendt's book, in the plight of refugees and ethnic minority populations in places such as Yugoslavia, Rwanda, and more recently in Kenya and Sudan.

According to Arendt, the Nazis exploited the discovery of the British Empire that 'only nationals could be citizens, only people of the same national origin could enjoy the full protection of legal institutions' (OT2: 155) to maximum effect. Arendt will claim in the third volume of her book that the genocide against the Jews began by taking away their full status as members of the German nation. This was the first and in some ways the most significant step towards their annihilation.

There is another aspect of bureaucratic rule that later became an important element of totalitarianism. Arendt claims that, by its nature, bureaucratic rule has no guiding principle, no political idea that determines the purpose of the government. In this it is unlike a democratically elected government, which usually defines its purpose in a written constitution. Without such a guiding idea, bureaucratic rule, according to Arendt, became about endless expansion of power for the sake of expansion:

> Bureaucracy was the organisation of the great game of expansion in which every area [of Africa] was considered a stepping stone to further involvements and every people an instrument for further conquest.
>
> (OT2: 66)

Arendt claims that in a state governed by bureaucracy, 'power, which in constitutional government only enforces the law, becomes the direct source of all legislation' (OT2: 123). According to Arendt, a certain type of power to commit legal acts of violence exists latently in a democratic state, where it serves the purpose of enforcing the law. This latent power is found in organs of the state such as the police and the judiciary, who are empowered to arrest, put on trial and punish those who break the law. Arendt claims that under the bureaucratic administration of the imperial territories, this latent force became the centre of all governing activity. Power, writes Arendt, 'became the essence of political action and the center of political thought when it was separated from the political community which it should serve' (OT2: 18). In other words, without a democratic public opinion of citizens to check on the way in which the state exercises its right to commit violence against those who break the law, the bureaucratic administrators of Africa were left free to resort to rule by sheer power and violence. Arendt writes in her essay *On Violence*, '[T]he greater the bureaucratization of public life, the greater will be the attraction of violence' (CR: 178).

These two aspects of bureaucratic rule, endless expansion and the rule of violence, became central to the totalitarian movements in power. In particular, Arendt thought that the politics of absolute power without responsibility found its ultimate expression in Adolf Eichmann, the archetypal Nazi bureaucrat (see Chapter 6). Strangely, Arendt is rather forgiving of the British Empire in comparison with the activities of the French, Germans and Belgians in Africa, writing that the British would never have dreamed of 'combining administration with massacre' (OT2: 66). Nevertheless, she argues that totalitarian bureaucracy was essentially a radicalisation of the discoveries of British rule in Africa.

Arendt is in some ways more explicit about the links between imperialism and totalitarianism than those between totalitarianism and anti-Semitism. The anti-Semitism of Paris at the end of the nineteenth century, in Arendt's account of it, fed in rather an amorphous way into the totalitarian psychology, with its attraction and repulsion towards Jews, as well as into the official anti-Semitic ideology of the Nazi party. Where Arendt's character study of Kurtz suggests to her that the blueprint for the Hitler personality was formed in the brutal lawlessness and power politics of imperial Africa, she thinks that the racial ideology and rule by bureaucracy evolved in this environment provide concrete historical templates for the realities of totalitarian rule and, in particular, for the Final Solution. There was a sense of infinite possibility for the colonial administrator in Africa, whose power was unhampered by the political institutions of the state which have traditionally put a check on the power of political leaders. Arendt describes the imperialist brutalisation of Africa and the total domination of the concentration camps in very similar terms. They are, for her, both worlds in which the infinite possibility for cruelty opened up by the loss of any laws, and any political realities at all, created a strange, surreal, twilight and fantastical world. Writing of the imperial adventures in Africa, she claims that 'what, after all, took decades to achieve in Europe, because of the delaying effect of social ethical values, exploded with the suddenness of a short circuit in the phantom world of colonial adventure' (OT2: 70). With the final breakdown of the nation-state in Europe, however, the brutal, phantom world of *Heart of Darkness* could make its appearance in the Nazi concentration camps.

CASE STUDY 8: ARENDT AND W.G. SEBALD

Before thinking a bit more about Arendt's account of the decline of the nation-state in Europe, it might be worthwhile to pause and ask whether Arendt's association of the imperial exploitation of Africa and Nazi totalitarian rule in Europe is entirely fanciful. The two phenomena are not connected with one another as often as they might be by historians of the twentieth century. But this might be to do with the way in which historical knowledge is carved up for specialised understanding by academics working on different historical events. Such specialisation often blinds us to the possible connections between those events. As we have seen, Arendt uses literary texts as a crucial alternative resource for thinking laterally about these connections.

W.G. Sebald's novel *Austerlitz* (2001) is a book about all kinds of things: architecture, memory, travel, the purpose of knowledge and different ways of seeing are some of its topics. But more than anything, *Austerlitz* is about the difficulty our culture has in remembering and bearing witness to an event as horrifying, traumatic and nearly incomprehensible as the Holocaust. Sebald approaches this issue through the story of one man's quest to find out about his origins. The novel begins in the waiting room of Antwerp railway station, in Belgium. The narrator notices the architectural extravagance of the building around him, including a 'verdigris-covered negro boy who, for a century now, has sat upon his dromedary on top of an oriel turret to the left of the station facade, a monument to the world of the animals and native peoples of the African continent, alone against the Flemish sky' (Sebald 2001: 4–5). Not long after this lonely image has been recorded, the narrator meets Austerlitz, a student of architecture, who explains to him why the railway station was built in such a lavish style by describing the time when it was built, the late nineteenth century,

> when Belgium, a little patch of yellowish grey barely visible on the map of the world, spread its sphere of influence to the African continent with its colonial enterprises, when deals of huge proportions were done on the capital markets and raw-materials exchanges of Brussels, and the citizens of Belgium, full of boundless optimism, believed their country […] was about to become a great new economic power.
>
> (Sebald 2001: 9)

It is striking that Sebald's novel, which is centrally preoccupied with the legacy and memory of Nazi rule in Europe, begins in a building which bears the memory of Belgium's imperial adventures in Africa and the fantastic wealth that these adventures generated for the citizens of Belgium. The grandeur of Antwerp railway station, claims Austerlitz, offers a little-acknowledged record of this period of Belgium's colonial activity. Perhaps in beginning a book which concerns itself with the Holocaust in this way, Sebald, like Arendt, is acknowledging the central connection between the histories of imperialism and totalitarian rule.

THE DECLINE OF THE NATION-STATE

A key argument of Arendt's work as a whole is that the human condition of plurality, the having of a 'world' shared in common, is a fragile state of affairs. This common world can easily be destroyed if its members do not choose to preserve it. Arendt thought that bourgeois society, with its commodity culture and its exploitation of Africa and Asia, had destroyed this common world. The member of the mob who became a brutal imperial adventurer in Africa, embodied by Conrad's Mr Kurtz, is the type of the human freed from all political bonds and licensed to pursue endless expansion of trade and profit unhampered by the rule of law. What happened in Africa was to be repeated in Europe under the totalitarian regimes. But in order for this to happen, the bourgeois idea of the state, which took its principles from the French Revolution, had to undergo a final collapse. This happened, according to Arendt, in the years after the First World War.

What imperialism and modern anti-Semitism both go to show is that a situation which is outside the law of the state, whether that situation be in the salons of Paris or on the plains of Africa, will always show man's capacity to commit unspeakable acts of brutality and domination over his fellow man. Arendt takes this as proof that the idea of natural rights enshrined in the principle of the French Revolution that, as Jean-Jacques Rousseau put it, man is 'born free', has been exposed as a lie by the experiences of modernity (see Chapter 1). There are no such things as natural human rights which belong to man from the moment of his birth. When men are taken out of a sphere of laws and publicly accountable institutions, the cruelty that they are capable of committing against one another shows that freedom and respect can be guaranteed only in a public realm which is fabricated by human endeavour. Arendt offers a sort of 'Lord of the Flies' argument, whereby men show their natural capacity for evil when they are released from the restraints of social conventions and laws. Arendt argues that human rights, 'supposedly inalienable, proved to be unenforceable [...] whenever people appeared who were no longer citizens of any sovereign state' (OT2: 173).

THE END OF THE RIGHTS OF MAN

Arendt claims that, in the modern world, political power and responsibility derive from the institution of the nation-state, a bounded and clearly defined territory, governed by constitutional law and populated by a community that recognises itself to have a common national identity, and whose members are protected by civil rights that claim to 'embody and spell out in the form of tangible laws the eternal Rights of Man'

(OT2: 173). Arendt also argues that the project of imperialist expansion stretched this definition of the nation-state to breaking point, by posing questions about the political constitution of an empire. The imperial adventures of the late nineteenth century opened up crucial constitutional issues such as whether the new populations and territories were to be incorporated into the nation-state or ruled over as 'protectorates'. Such issues challenged the traditional basis of the nation-state as a political entity that is territorially bounded and populated by a common nation. Even more fundamentally, imperialist expansion stretched to breaking point the principle of consent on which the nation-state was founded. According to this principle, the population of a nation are understood to have a social contract with their government, whereby they consent, as law-abiding citizens, to be ruled over by a government that agrees in return to guarantee their personal freedom and to protect their private property. But the populations of the new empires had hardly 'chosen' to be ruled over.

Arendt describes how in Europe after the First World War an equivalent situation to that in imperialist Africa emerged. After the war, a number of populations across Europe existed in an uneasy condition in newly formed nation-states such as Czechoslovakia, Hungary and Yugoslavia. These states had been formed out of the break-up of the Ottoman, German and Austro-Hungarian empires that had previously dominated continental European power politics, but that were on the losing side in the war. The new states were designed to be fairly ethnically homogeneous entities, but inevitably, given the cultural diversity of Europe, many of them contained minority populations. Arendt thinks of the minority populations as roughly analogous to the African and Asian populations that had been annexed by the imperialists of the nineteenth century. By rights, both types of population should have found themselves under the protection of the nation-state, but in practice they found themselves cruelly exposed. Like the subjects of the British, French, German, Italian and Belgian empires before them, and like refugees and displaced persons in the twenty-first century, minority populations within Europe at this time were exposed to a very precarious and uncertain position within the political community that hosted them. Their safety was supposedly guaranteed by international law, but in practice this concept turned out to be something of a toothless lion.

'THE RIGHT TO HAVE RIGHTS'

Arendt argues that the experience of the minority populations created by the First World War had exposed a hitherto hidden pre-condition of rights bearing within the nation-state. This is, that the nation-state itself granted the individual the right to have rights, rather than serving to protect and guarantee rights which inhere 'naturally' in the individual. Rights are the work of the state, but can be guaranteed only by the existence of a genuine political community. This means that when the critical public opinion of a nation chooses to look the other way, that state might take away the rights of some of those who live within its borders.

To ask why it was that Jews went so submissively to their deaths in the gas chambers is to fundamentally misapprehend the way that the Nazis' exploitation of the ambiguities in the concept of human rights had already made resistance seem futile. Having taken away legal personhood from the Jews, and then taken away their homes and possessions, their place in the world, Arendt claims that the Nazis found it easier than they had anticipated to take away the moral person that might have resisted his annihilation, and therefore to drive this person without resistance into the gas chambers.

Arendt's argument underlines both how crucial constitutional law is to guaranteeing civic and moral human identity, and how easy it has been in the modern world to take these identities away. The sad truth is that 'a man who is nothing but a man has lost the very qualities which make it possible for other people to treat him as a fellow-man' (OT2: 180). She finds the question of how human beings could be reduced to the status of cattle for the slaughter easier to answer than the question of how others in a republic who were spared this fate could let it happen to their fellow citizens. Rights, whether as civic rights, or the so-called 'rights of man' can only really exist if they are framed by a genuine political community.

CONCLUSIONS

It is important to bear in mind in setting out on a reading of *The Origins of Totalitarianism* that Arendt's own life-story was heavily determined by the kinds of social experience that she discusses in her book. In particular, Arendt's early life as a German Jew was heavily determined by the disintegration of traditional forms of social organisation in Europe between the two world wars, as the fragmentation of the old European empires into nation-states gave rise to a new tribal politics. The kind of tribal nationalism and ethnic conflict that erupted in Eastern Europe when Arendt was growing up is now an all too familiar feature of our own world in the light of the ethnic conflicts in Yugoslavia (which date back to the period that Arendt discusses in her book) and Rwanda in the 1990s, and the more recent sectarian and racial violence in Iraq and Darfur. In *The Origins of Totalitarianism*, Arendt's political and historical writing is then also partly autobiographical.

Arendt's reading of literary texts is a crucial part of her analysis of the elements of totalitarianism, as can be seen from her use of Proust to think about the formation of modern anti-Semitism (see Chapter 6). In the 'Imperialism' volume of her book, Arendt reads Joseph Conrad's novel *Heart of Darkness* as an exploration of how a terrifying new racial ideology was formulated in the exploitation of Africa by the European imperial powers. This racial ideology was new because it legitimised the mass extermination of racial groups. Arendt claims that this racial ideology was later appropriated by the Nazis and that, consequently, literary texts such as Conrad's offer crucial resources for thinking about the origins of totalitarian racism. She also claims that imperialism provided new types of political experience and forms of rule that could be appropriated by the Nazis, and in particular the experience of rule by bureaucracy. These experiences of imperialism and home-grown anti-Semitism were fused in the totalitarian movements, which sprang out of the failure of the bourgeois idea of the nation-state.

8

TOTALITARIANISM

The third volume of *The Origins of Totalitarianism* is concerned with the genesis, ideology and practices of the totalitarian movements of the Soviet Union and Germany. In it Arendt produces some of the most powerful, radically original and disturbing writing of her whole career. As with the first two volumes of the study, this volume is essentially an exercise in understanding totalitarianism. Arendt asks, in the introduction to the 1966 edition of her book, '*What happened? Why did it happen? How could it have happened?*' (OT3: vi).

Arendt's study of totalitarianism is not, however, simply an historical survey of a phenomenon that came to an end with the death of Hitler. In the third volume of *Origins*, Arendt works with both the past and present tenses. In the use of the past tense, Arendt seeks to tell the story of how Nazi and Soviet totalitarianism had become possible, but her use of the present tense suggests that totalitarianism remains a problem for the modern world (not least because Stalin was still ruling the Soviet Union when Arendt's book was first published). Totalitarianism had, according to Arendt, experimented with 'the permanent domination of each single individual in each and every sphere of life' (OT3: 24). More terrifyingly still, according to Arendt totalitarianism had discovered methods to make people active agents in their own oppression.

CONTRADICTION

Arendt's task in the third volume of her book is to make intelligible a world that had lost all meaning, a world in which, as she wrote in an essay in 1954, 'common sense' had broken down (EU: 314). But this is a very difficult thing to do. The Nazi and Soviet totalitarian movements were, according to Arendt, inherently contradictory. There was no consistency to their actions, and so any attempt to 'make sense' of those actions is liable to overestimate the extent to which there was any meaning or rationale to them.

FASCINATION

Arendt plunges her readers headlong into a sense of totalitarianism's contradictions at the beginning of the third volume of her book. She starts out by thinking about the charismatic personalities of the totalitarian leaders, Hitler and Stalin, and the 'fascination' that they held for society. The subject of the 'charisma' of the totalitarian personality preoccupied sociologists, historians and critical theorists in the years after the war. For example, a year before Arendt's book was published, a group of American sociologists and German émigré critical theorists published a psychological study, *Authoritarian Personality (Studies in Prejudice)*. Arendt was fairly hostile to the attempt to 'psychologise' the nature of totalitarian politics, which she thought overestimated the role of the totalitarian leaders in the development of the movements. However, she begins her book with a brief response to the contemporary interest in the nature of the totalitarian personality. Arendt describes how Hitler 'exercised a fascination to which allegedly no one was immune' (OT3: 3). She had already described fascination as a key component of the proto-totalitarian personality of the imperialist adventurer, and in particular of Mr Kurtz in Joseph Conrad's *Heart of Darkness* (see Chapter 7). According to Arendt, Hitler's fascination was a 'social phenomenon' that derived from his absolute refusal to ever adapt his ideas to changing circumstances. She writes the following in a footnote:

> In modern society, with its characteristic lack of discerning judgment, this tendency [towards fascination] is strengthened, so that someone who not only holds opinions but also presents them in a tone of unshakable conviction will

> not so easily forfeit his prestige, no matter how many times he has been demonstrably wrong […] The hair-raising arbitrariness of such fanaticism holds great fascination for society because for the duration of the social gathering it is freed from the chaos of opinions that it constantly generates.
>
> (OT3: 3)

Hitler, argues Arendt, was the product of a society that had lost the ability to make meaningful moral and political judgements. She claims that it was not the content of what Hitler said that fascinated his contemporaries, but the fact that he was prepared to stick to his opinions no matter how often he was proved wrong and no matter how out of touch with reality he could be shown to be. To this extent, Arendt implies, Hitler could have been saying almost anything and still have generated fascination, because the purpose he really served was to offer a way out of society itself and 'the chaos of opinions that it constantly generates'. It is the absurd and terrifying consistency of Hitler's pronouncements, rather than what he actually said, that explains his effect on others. What Hitler offered was, according to Arendt, an escape from the very need to have 'opinions' or to make judgements at all, the prerequisites of any meaningful social life.

The idea that totalitarianism proposed an escape from society uncovers a fundamental, destructive and nihilistic aspect of the totalitarian movements. Totalitarianism, according to Arendt, broke with the Western tradition by abandoning the very idea that there is meaning in what we say, that the opinions that we hold in public have any internal content or consistency. It is of the essence of public opinion, classically defined, to be open to the views of others and to their attempts at persuasion, and to be subject to change in the light of new information or a shift in world view brought on by contact with others. In maintaining his opinions unchanged, no matter how inconsistent with reality they might be shown to be, Hitler denied this fundamental aspect of the human condition of plurality (see Chapter 2). Totalitarianism's abandonment of a fundamental premise of thinking and acting in the Western tradition then presents a major difficulty in the attempt to understand it. In particular, it is difficult to see how it could ever become possible to understand and to make sense of the totalitarian movements if, as Arendt implies, the totalitarian leader thought of his own ideas and ideologies as meaningless vehicles for the authority of his personality.

Arendt claims, however, that it is important not to be taken in by Hitler's rhetoric. To assume that there is any consistency or meaning to totalitarian policy is, according to Arendt, to have already succumbed to the fascination of Hitler. In fact, Arendt claims, the apparent consistency in the opinions of the totalitarian leader is an illusion. She writes that 'if there is such a thing as a totalitarian personality or mentality', then 'an extraordinary adaptability and absence of continuity are no doubt its outstanding characteristics' (OT3: 4). Far from being a completely self-sufficient and ruthlessly consistent ideology, as Hitler's speeches and writing would lead one to believe, Arendt claims that totalitarianism is actually endlessly self-contradictory, and that there is in fact no continuity to anything that the totalitarian leader does or says.

CASE STUDY 9: TOTALITARIAN 'MOVEMENTS': ARENDT AND GEORGE ORWELL

In an essay which he wrote in 1946 called 'The Prevention of Literature', the English essayist, novelist and political thinker George Orwell (1903–50) made the following startling claim about totalitarianism:

> What is new in totalitarianism is that its doctrines are not only unchallengeable but also unstable. They have to be accepted on pain of damnation, but on the other hand they are always liable to be altered at a moment's notice.
>
> (Orwell 2003: 217)

No doubt Arendt would agree entirely with Orwell's insight into the contradiction deep at the heart of totalitarianism. Totalitarian ideology claims to be absolutely self-consistent and immovable, but in reality it is liable to radically transform itself whenever such a transformation suits its needs. According to both Arendt and Orwell, totalitarianism creates an environment in which human action is stripped of any possible meaning.

MOVEMENT

Arendt makes the difficult claim that there was no meaning to the actions and ideologies of the Nazis, nor of other totalitarian movements, and that in fact the only aim of the movements was to keep moving, and in particular to became more and more powerful and more and more destructive. In order to achieve this endless destructive expansion, the totalitarian movements had to dismantle the political structure of the state, which might have put checks on their destructive ambitions:

> One should not forget that only a building can have a structure, but that a movement – if the word is to be taken as seriously and as literally as the Nazis meant it – can have only a direction, and that any form of legal or governmental structure can be only a handicap to a movement which is being propelled with increasing speed in a certain direction.

> (OT3: 96)

Arendt argues that these movements were, however, clever enough to realise that the populations that they ruled over needed to *believe* that there was a principle or idea governing the movement, and to persuade their supporters that the movement had an ultimate goal. Totalitarian propaganda, as expounded in Hitler's and Stalin's speeches and pronouncements, gave the movement the veneer of consistency that its actual practices completely undermined.

FROM THE MOB TO THE MASS

In order to understand the origins of totalitarianism, Arendt thought that it was particularly important to pay attention to the way that the totalitarian movements had exploited the breakdown in European society that had been brought on by commodity capitalism, imperialism and the First World War. In particular, Arendt claims that crucial to the Nazis' seizure of power was the way that they functioned as a 'mass movement'. Arendt claims that the totalitarian leaders exercised a particular fascination on two social groups: the masses and the intellectuals. Arendt understands the mass as a direct descendent of the 'mob' of the late nineteenth century (see Chapter 7). The mob had been a 'surplus' product of bourgeois society, and had lived off that society's drive for expansion, in particular by trying its fortune in imperial adventures overseas. According to Arendt, the mob was radicalised into a mass by the experiences of the First World War. Where the mob had functioned as a kind of surplus to the bourgeoisie, Arendt argues that the masses had become violently hostile, as a result of their war experiences, to the values of bourgeois society, which were increasingly seen by this new mass as 'society's humanitarian and liberal hypocrisy' (OT3: 29). But this is not to say that the mass rejected the experience of the war or that its protest against bourgeois hypocrisy led it into pacificism or an anti-war movement. According to Arendt, the mass understood the horror and brutality of the trenches as the real essence of human existence. 'War,' writes Arendt, 'with its constant murderous arbitrariness, became the symbol for death, the "great equaliser" and therefore the true father of a new world order' (OT3: 27). War seemed to the mass to found a new world order because its horror and death were real, authentic and not the product of illusory bourgeois sentiment.

MASS 'WORLD ALIENATION'

Where the mob had been parasitic on bourgeois society, the mass became actively hostile towards the bourgeoisie, and wanted to destroy what it saw as its phoney respectability. Where the mob was opportunist and adventurous, and essentially egotistical, the mass was highly ideological and 'selfless'. It wanted, in fact, to destroy society, and it was prepared to go to any lengths in order to achieve that destruction. So fanatical was the mass in its hatred of bourgeois society, and so uprooted by its war experience, that it even gave up on the basic human desire for self-preservation. 'Selflessness', argues Arendt, became a 'mass phenomenon' (OT3: 13). Arendt claims that individual 'mass men' wanted to lose themselves in the wider identity of the mass movements. But this is not to say that the masses, in their selflessness, became concerned for others, which would be one definition of 'selflessness'. Rather, argues Arendt, the masses considered the lives of everyone, including their own, to be equally expendable. Any claim to care for others, any expression of 'pity' or 'sympathy' for others, became evidence of a residual bourgeois ideology that had to be ruthlessly annihilated. This total annihilation of any social feeling, the sense in the mass man not only that he is expendable but that everyone around him is expendable too, prepared the ground crucially for the Nazi movement.

THE MASSES AND AL QAEDA?

A number of commentators have recently sought to compare Arendt's analysis of totalitarianism and mass mentality to contemporary Islamic fundamentalism and terrorism (Young-Bruehl 2004; Power 2006). The fanatical 'mass man', like the Al Qaeda operative, say such analysts, has completely lost any sense of selfhood, and has instead become fixated on an ideological goal that must be achieved even if the whole human race is to be wiped out in the process. Both movements also rely on the use of terror as a political weapon. Yet such efforts at understanding totalitarianism in a contemporary light offer rather speculative and politically worrying analogies. In particular, they risk reinforcing the ideological agenda of neoconservatism, which in recent years has conflated Islamic fundamentalism with the Nazis in the horribly trite claim that Al Qaeda are 'Islamic fascists' or that there is such a thing as 'Islamofascism'. This is not to say that Arendt's work is irrelevant to the current global situation. The last section of this book will look at some of the ways in which her work is in fact indispensable to current efforts to analyse the 'war on terror'. Before doing that, though, it would seem to be far more sensible to contextualise Arendt's work on mass society in her own historical moment.

THE INTELLECTUALS AND THE MASSES

The hatred of the masses for bourgeois society is echoed in Martin Heidegger's hostility, in his book *Being and Time*, to the 'idle talk' of the public, as well as his attempt to reinvest death with a real meaning, against the 'forgetfulness' of society about this fundamental condition of being (see Chapter 4). In fact one aspect of the interwar years that Arendt found particularly troubling was the attraction of the intellectual elite of Germany, France and England to the new mass movements. Arendt describes 'the terrifying roster of distinguished men whom totalitarianism can count among its sympathizers, fellow-travelers, and inscribed party members' (OT3: 24). She suggests in particular that European artists and intellectuals were attracted to the assault of the mass on bourgeois 'respectability', and the claim of the masses that cruelty and destruction were more honest, less hypocritical forms of human interaction than bourgeois society could offer. There is certainly evidence of a new fascination with cruelty and violence in the work of the artistic avant-garde of this period, for example in the work of the French writer and thinker Georges Bataille (1897–1962) and the dramatist and theorist of the 'theatre of cruelty' Antonin Artaud (1896–1948). (This is not to say that Bataille or Artaud were

Nazi sympathisers.) Arendt claims that the alliance between the mass and the artistic and intellectual elite went across the political divide between left and right, since authors who were sympathetic to Hitlerian and Stalinist totalitarianism had a common hatred for the bourgeoisie.

The idea of mass society preoccupied artists and social theorists in the early twentieth century. A key study of this phenomenon was Gustave Le Bon's *The Crowd* (first published in 1895). There is a distinction to be drawn, however, between Arendt's attitude towards the masses and those of some of her contemporaries in the English-speaking world. In England, the relation between the masses and the intellectuals in the 1920s and 1930s is generally thought to have been a much more oppositional one than the one that Arendt suggests. In his book *The Intellectuals and the Masses* (1992), the English literary critic John Carey describes the whole of modernist literary writing in English as a revolt against the new phenomenon of 'mass culture' in England. According to Carey, the difficulty and obscurity of poets such as T.S. Eliot and of novelists such as Virginia Woolf is the result of a self-conscious attempt to exclude a whole new mass of lower middle class readers, who had benefited from educational reform in late nineteenth-century England and were using it to try to 'better themselves', much to the irritation of modernist intellectuals. When Eliot describes a 'crowd' flowing over London Bridge in his 1922 poem 'The Waste Land' (see Chapter 5), he does so with a distinct air of disapproval for this particular mass of humanity. Yet Arendt's own attitude to the mass is less hostile. She even at times comes close to identifying with the anti-bourgeois sentiment of the masses, writing at one point in *The Origins of Totalitarianism* of 'how justified disgust can be in a society wholly permeated with the ideological outlook and moral standards of the bourgeoisie' (OT3: 26). The English masses wanted to become respectable and bourgeois, according to Carey, and this is why the English intelligentsia became so prejudiced against them. But the continental masses had reached a much more nihilistic, anti-bourgeois state of development.

According to Arendt, Nazism did not really speak for the masses. Rather, it exploited them in its drive for destruction. Having exploited both the masses and the intellectuals, Hitler then abandoned them to the destruction that, he argued, they had willed on themselves. This betrayal is particularly pronounced in the case of the intellectuals.

Nazism may have fascinated figures such as Heidegger, but Nazism and Stalinism ultimately revealed themselves to be profoundly anti-intellectual. Arendt quotes a senior Nazi as saying 'when I hear the word culture, I draw my revolver' (OT3: 26), which gives a good sense of the real attitude of the Nazis to the intellectuals. Ultimately, Arendt claims, whenever totalitarian movements seized power, 'this whole group of sympathizers was shaken off even before the regimes proceeded toward their greatest crimes' (OT3: 37). The same goes for Russia as for Germany, where intellectuals were quickly weeded out from society in Stalin's purges.

CASE STUDY 10: 1984

How can we begin to make sense of life in a totalitarian environment, when that environment has wilfully abandoned all meaningful and self-consistent definitions of reality? This case study will mount a comparative reading of *The Origins of Totalitarianism* and George Orwell's novel *1984* (published in 1949), in order to place Arendt's study of life in a totalitarian environment in a context that will be more familiar to readers from a literary studies background.

The first two volumes of Arendt's book draw on literary examples in order to recover the social experiences of anti-Semitism and imperialist racism, and also as a way of understanding how these experiences later fed into the totalitarian movements. The third volume of Arendt's book attempts to make sense of the experience of life in a totalitarian state. Here, for obvious reasons, Arendt had very little literary writing to draw on in her effort to imagine what it must have been like to live in Nazi Germany or in Stalinist Russia. Life under a totalitarian regime became, in a certain sense, 'fictional', in that the ruling party made use of a powerful mixture of ideology and terror in order to redefine what 'reality' is, and to silence any possible opposition to this official version of reality. In the time since Arendt published her book, this control of reality under totalitarian regimes has been examined by a number of fiction writers who had had first-hand experience of life under totalitarianism. Examples include the work of Milan Kundera (1929–), the Czech author of *The Unbearable Lightness of Being* (1984), and the Russian author Alexander Solzhenitsyn (1918–), whose novel *The First Circle*, according to Arendt, 'contains the best documentation on Stalin's regime in existence' (CR: 154). Such literary accounts of Soviet-style totalitarianism are matched by a vast array of memoirs produced by survivors of the Nazi death camps, such as Primo Levi, a survivor of Auschwitz, and Jorge Semprun (1923–), a survivor of Buchenwald. There is a powerful link to be drawn between totalitarianism and writing, in that totalitarianism has often oppressed freedom of artistic expression in its attempt to 'author' reality itself, and in that some of the writers listed above have sought to 'write back' against this definitive, totalitarian view of reality. Arendt's study of totalitarianism can be usefully understood as an equivalent attempt to resist the totalitarian domination and distortion of reality.

Orwell's novel, too, begins with just such an act of resistance. Its hero, Winston Smith, resists the authority of the totalitarian regime that he lives under and works for by writing a diary. The novel is set in a dystopian future in which England, now named 'Airstrip 1' and part of a new superpower called 'Oceania', is under the total domination of 'Big Brother' and his party. Smith struggles to resist the totalitarian regime because everything he knows about himself and his history, apart from a few untrustworthy and faded memories, has been fed to him by Big Brother. Orwell's novel gives a subtle sense of the loneliness and alienation of a life in which all information about the past, present and future has been fabricated by a governmental authority.

For Arendt, feelings of loneliness in the socially dislocated individual explain the attraction of mass movements. She writes that the masses 'grew out of the fragments of a highly atomized society whose competitive structure and concomitant loneliness of the individual had been held in check only through membership in a class' (OT3: 15). Rather than finding a sense of belonging in the mass movement, however, Arendt argues that totalitarian rule transformed the mass man's sense of loneliness into a condition of complete isolation. The deployment of propaganda and the use of terror as a political weapon left the individual under totalitarianism permanently uncertain as to whether he was thinking the 'right' thoughts, and whether those thoughts were shared by others. Effectively, totalitarian rule collapsed any possibility of a social community in which it might be possible to recognise and to communicate with others.

Orwell explores some of the same experiences of totalitarian rule in his novel. He describes, through the character of Winston Smith, how totalitarian propaganda works to suck up the individual into a condition of mass hysteria, while simultaneously making him feel isolated.

Smith is forced to play the part of a dedicated servant of the party, to the point where play-acting has become almost instinctive. 'To dissemble your feelings,' writes Orwell, 'to control your face, to do what everyone else was doing, was an instinctive reaction' (Orwell 1983: 752). But Smith's awareness that he is constantly playing a part does not save him from being caught up in the mass movement. When he is exposed to Big Brother's propaganda, he notes that 'it was impossible to avoid joining in' (Orwell 1983: 750) with a mass expression of hate against portrayals of the 'Enemy of the People'. Smith loses his sense of self in this mass sentiment of hatred.

PROPAGANDA

As well as loneliness, fear is a primary part of the experience of life in a totalitarian state for both of Orwell and Arendt. This fear comes partly from totalitarian propaganda, which portrays the world beyond the reach of the totalitarian movement as hostile to its ambitions, in order to draw the individual into commitment to the movement. The totalitarian organisation therefore 'prevents its members ever being directly confronted with the outside world' (OT3: 65) by allowing them access only to distorted representations of the non-totalitarian world. Arendt describes how totalitarian propaganda functions by cutting its recipients off from reality, from the common world, in order to prepare them to accept the insane and contradictory programme of the movement itself. For Orwell, totalitarian propaganda works best on those who have already lost their status as public actors:

> In a way, the world view of the Party imposed itself most successfully on people incapable of understanding it. They could be made to accept the most flagrant violations of reality, because they never fully grasped the enormity of what was demanded of them, and were not sufficiently interested in public events to notice what was happening. By lack of understanding they remained sane.
>
> (Orwell 1983: 836)

POLICE STATE

Arendt had claimed in the second volume of her book that Nazi bureaucracy 'intruded upon the private individual and his inner life with equal brutality' (OT2: 125). The major organ of this state-run distortion of reality was the police, which sought to control the thoughts and sentiments of the 'citizens' by keeping them in a perpetual state of terror (in Orwell's dystopian future, there is a separate police force for controlling the inner lives of individuals, called the 'Thought Police'). Totalitarianism built on and radicalised the imperialist practice of basing government exclusively on the state's organs of violence, the police and the bureaucracy (see Chapter 7). Arendt argues that the police force was not just an important tool for the exercise of totalitarian power, but that this claim also works the other way around to the extent that totalitarianism actually exists for the sake of the police. Arendt's understanding of the surreal, counterfactual nature of totalitarian rule thus leads her to her own highly counter-intuitive insights:

> The Nazis did not think that the Germans were a master race, to whom the world belonged, but that they should be led by a master race, as should all other nations, and that this race was only on the point of being born. Not the Germans were the dawn of the master race, but the SS.

(OT3: 110)

Arendt claims that the SS was not simply an organ of the Nazi state, but that they were actually its *raison d'être*. (Although the SS had originally been a part of the Nazi party, Arendt argues that it had gradually overtaken the secret police or Gestapo over the course of the Nazi regime, to become the police force itself (OT3: 78).) The Nazi state was then a police state, according to Arendt, not only in the sense that it was run by the police, but also in that it was run for the police. Relatedly, Arendt claims that the Nazis were suspicious of the army, which they thought might still be subject to old-style German nationalism. The nation-state, for the Nazis, was just another barrier to their drive for endless destruction which must be overcome. They made use of old-style German nationalism to hoodwink the people into the movement, but in fact, according to Arendt, the Nazis were profoundly internationalist in outlook, and scathing about nationalist politics.

This idea of the Nazis' internationalism also gives a different view of the role of anti-Semitism in Nazi propaganda. Arendt argues that the perceived 'internationalism' of Jews, the fact that Jewish businesses and families often existed and operated across state boundaries, was something that the Nazis, in their resistance to the state, actually sought to emulate. This seems like a hugely counter-intuitive, and potentially offensive claim to make; nevertheless, Arendt was persuaded that the 'delusion of an already existing Jewish world domination formed the basis for the illusion of future German world domination' (OT3: 58). As with so much of her writing on the history of the relations between Nazi totalitarianism and the Jews, the claim that the Nazis wanted to emulate the perceived organisation of the Jews is uncomfortable, and potentially controversial.

CONCENTRATION CAMPS

At the symbolic centre of the Nazi police state, argued Arendt, is found the detention and destruction of human beings in the concentration camps. Arendt was interested in the extent to which what went on in the concentration camps was a hidden or 'secret' centre of the movement. In the course of her analysis of totalitarian rule, Arendt claims to uncover an inverse relation between power and secrecy. In other words, the more powerful the Nazi movement became, the more secretive it became about its real goals. Again, this seems to be a paradoxical and contradictory position to hold in that secrecy would, logically speaking, be used by a political organisation that lacks power and therefore needs to hide its real intentions. Arendt then points to the paradoxical conclusion that the Nazi secret services were expanded further and further when there was no one left to spy on. She writes that '[o]nly after the extermination of real enemies has been completed and the hunt for 'objective enemies' begun does terror become the actual content of totalitarian regimes' (OT3: 120). Arendt understood the concentration camps as sites of pure terror, where the absolutely powerless are confronted with the absolutely powerful in a situation which finally destroys any notion of a human condition in which power is the product of human interaction.

Arendt was convinced that this loss of humanity, and not any practical or utilitarian purpose, was the real object of the concentration camps. 'The incredibility of the horrors', she writes, 'is closely bound up with their economic uselessness' (OT3: 143). The camps were the space in which the totalitarian rulers tested the reach of their destructive drives, 'the indecent experimental inquiry into what is possible' (OT3: 134). They performed, in other words, a kind of scientific experiment, a testing out of the limits of the human condition and the extent to which that condition could be destroyed. The genocide committed by the Nazis against the Jews brought about a gigantic destruction of life-stories, which operated by depriving death of its cultural meaning: 'The concentration camps, by making death itself anonymous [...] robbed death of its meaning as the end of a fulfilled life' (OT3: 150). In essence, the camps functioned as a form of counter-society, 'the only form of society in which it is possible to dominate man entirely' (OT3: 154). In Arendt's highly metaphorical understanding of the concentration camps, the actions of the Nazis constitute a kind of scientific 'experiment' to discover not only whether everyone can be killed, but also whether the humanity in individual human beings can be destroyed.

CONCLUSIONS

Arendt's analysis of the concentration camps reinforces what she argues about the nature of totalitarian propaganda: that any attempt to discern a purpose or rational idea behind the actions of the move-ment has itself succumbed to Nazi propaganda. Rather, what that propaganda exposes is the *dissimulation* of purpose, meaning and use-fulness in order to cover up the absolutely nihilistic destructiveness and domination that is the principle of action of the Nazi regime. The camps are the centre of this, and in them is crystallised the essence of totalitar-ianism itself. Towards the end of her book, Arendt writes the following:

> What totalitarian ideologies [...] aim at is not the transformation of the outside world or the revolutionizing transmutation of society, but the transformation of human nature itself. The concentration camps are the laboratories where changes in human nature are tested, and their shamefulness therefore is not just the business of their inmates and those who run them according to strictly "scientific" standards; it is the concern of all men.
>
> (OT3: 156)

Arendt's telling of the tragic story of modernity, which begins with the promise of a new reconciliation between thinking and acting opened up by Kant's political philosophy, ends with the victim of the con-centration camp, a bundle of reactions who, she says, constitutes the 'ideal citizen' of the totalitarian 'state'.

CODA: EVIL

Many critical accounts of Arendt's work have focused on her various discussions of the concept of evil. Yet in some ways evil is a fairly marginal and problematic term for Arendt. In a postscript to *Eichmann in Jerusalem*, the book which she subtitled *A Report on the Banality of Evil,* Arendt emphasised the 'report' element of her writing, claiming that it had been intended as a study of 'a man of flesh and blood with an individual history', and that it was 'least of all' intended as 'a theoretical treatise on the nature of evil' (EJ: 285). Nevertheless, this is an area of Arendt's thought that has been most consistently over- and misinterpreted. Arendt was accused at the time of publication of sloganising with her phrase 'the banality of evil', as if her idea of evil were superficial and intended to be eye-catching. In fact, Arendt did think of modern, totalitarian evil as a 'superficial' phenomenon. This brief coda will examine just what is at stake in this claim of Arendt's.

Arendt often approached the question of evil by thinking about literary representations of evil. In her postscript to the Eichmann trial she compared Eichmann, for example, to Shakespeare's Richard III (EJ: 287). In her essay *On Revolution*, published in the same year as the Eichmann book, Arendt considered the question of evil in Herman Melville's story *Billy Budd* where she locates 'evil beyond vice' in Melville's portrayal of the villainous Claggart. Here, Arendt understood 'absolute evil' (OR: 84) and absolute goodness or innocence as equivalent, anti-political or pre-political forces that exist outside of law. Arendt shows in her reading of the story how goodness and innocence can cause as much destruction and violence to the political community as can evil. Her comparative analysis of the figure of evil (Claggart) and the figure of good (Billy Budd) intends to disturb and question ideological representations of the human being, and of human nature, as either innately good or innately evil.

In an essay from 1946 on the novelist Hermann Broch, 'No Longer and Not Yet', Arendt wrote that 'the death factories [i.e. concentration camps] erected in the heart of Europe definitely cut the already out-worn thread with which we still might have been tied to a historical entity of more than two thousand years' (Arendt 2007b: 122). Arendt claims, in effect, that the experience of the concentration camps brought about a definitive break with the whole history of Western Europe and its systems of values and norms. Yet Arendt fell back on one of the oldest and most traditional ideas, the theological category of evil, in order to describe the concentration camps in *The Origins of Totalitarianism*. She writes there that 'the reality of concentration camps resembles nothing so much as medieval pictures of Hell' (OT3: 145), and describes the actions of those who organised them as an 'absolute evil which could no longer be understood and explained by the evil motives of self-interest, greed, covetousness, resentment, lust for power, and cowardice' (OT3: 157). How can these two different interpretations be reconciled? How can the concentration camps at once bring about a break with tradition, and be comprehended with reference to perhaps the oldest, most traditional theological category that there is, evil?

ABSOLUTE EVIL

One explanation for Arendt's appeal to the category of evil in her analysis of totalitarianism would be to understand it as testament to the exhaustion of all philosophical or sociological standards by which the actions of responsible agents could be judged. In *The Origins of Totalitarianism*, Arendt describes how the philosophical tradition has never been able to conceive of 'radical evil'. The use of the word 'radical' here indicates a type of evil which is deep within the human being as part of his nature, and the term 'radical evil' derives from a medieval Christian understanding of the human being. The philosophical tradition sought to depart from this notion of man as naturally evil, a kind of 'fallen' being who is already a sinner at birth. For Kant, writes Arendt, the phenomenon of evil is only the manifestation of 'a perverted ill-will' (OT3: 157). For Kant, in other words, man is not predisposed in his nature to commit evil acts, but rather evil is the product of a good will which has become perverted. But Arendt claims that the concentration camps had changed human nature to such an extent that they had, in effect, reinvented this phenomenon of radical evil. Radical evil, she writes, 'has emerged in connection with a system in which all men have become equally superfluous' (OT3: 157). The camps, in other words, had undone the philosophical tradition. In order to understand this definitive break with the philosophical tradition, Arendt seems to say, we need to revert to an older, metaphysical or religious notion of radical evil. There is no other way to make sense of a system of absolute degradation in which human life has lost all value and become 'superfluous'.

THE BANALITY OF EVIL

In an essay written in 1943 on the concentration camps, Arendt claimed that 'hell is no longer a religious belief or a fantasy, but something as real as houses and stones and trees' (JW: 265). But Arendt's response to the Eichmann trial twenty years later suggests that she changed her mind about evil. In particular, her study of Eichmann appears to have taken her back in-line with the philosophical tradition, and back to a view of man as a being capable of doing evil deeds but not in himself inherently evil. The doing of evil deeds in the modern world did not seem to Arendt to be the product of some deep, inner or innate impulse. Rather, evil had become institutionalised, depersonalised and mundane. To many of Arendt's readers, the claim about Eichmann's 'banality' seemed to excuse him from responsibility for his deeds, but in fact Arendt wanted to do nothing of the sort. Rather, it was precisely the banality of Eichmann's evil that she found terrifying. Her message is that the mundane, the banal, can have a profound effect on the world. In the controversy that followed the publication of her book, Arendt tried to capture this peculiar and paradoxical quality of a depthless evil by analogy with a natural process. In her response to a letter from a former acquaintance, Gershom

Scholem, who had accused her of sloganising with her phrase 'the banality of evil', Arendt argued that evil has the superficial, corrupting quality of natural decay:

> It is indeed my opinion now that evil is never "radical", that it is only extreme, and that it possesses neither depth nor any demonic dimension. It can over-grow and lay waste the whole world precisely because it spreads like a fungus on the surface. It is "thought-defying", as I said, because thought tries to reach some depth, to go to the roots, and the moment it concerns itself with evil, it is frustrated because there is nothing. That is its "banality".

(JW: 471)

Natural forces can be banal, superficial in themselves, but capable of great devastation – like a fungus, which might rot the framework of a house. We need to understand the 'banality of evil' as a figure, a metaphor which is intended to cope with a reality that no longer makes sense – and also to understand it in relation to the under-standing of nature that Arendt outlined in *The Human Condition*. Arendt wrote in reply to the accusation that she underestimated Eichmann's crimes that 'Nothing could be further from my mind than to trivialize the greatest catastrophe of our century' (JW: 487). But balanced against this need to bear witness to the enormity of the Nazi crimes, Arendt also felt a duty to report on their meaninglessness and superficiality. It takes a great deal of tact to capture a phenomenon that is both unprecedented in terms of its horror and banal in the way that it carries out that horror, and perhaps Arendt did, indeed, lack the necessary tact in dealing with this problem.

Arendt wanted to avoid the danger of reinvesting the horror of the Holocaust with metaphysical meaning, while explaining the full destructive force of its superficiality. The difficulties that Arendt faced in trying to represent the unrepresentable are not unique to her. Some scholars prefer to use the Hebrew term 'shoah' rather than 'holocaust' to describe the Nazi genocide. A 'holocaust' among the ancient Jews was a burnt sacrifice offered to God in the temple of Jerusalem, and it might arguably be an inappropriate term to use to describe the genocide, since the notion of sacrifice implies exchange, symbolic meaning and, ultimately, redemption. In the Nazi genocide there was no exchange and no meaning to the mass annihilation – it was never a 'sacrifice', which would imply that something was gained from all the suffering.

In the same way, Arendt wants us to face up to the absolute emptiness of the Jewish suffering.

But why, then, hold on to this term 'evil'? Why not just get rid of it altogether? Was it, as some of Arendt's critics suggested, a 'slogan'? Perhaps Arendt's use of the word evil serves to mark the place where there was once meaning, but there is no more.

AFTER ARENDT

> The banality of evil [...] Have the grand Lucifers of Dante and Milton been retired for good, their place taken by a pack of dusty little demons that perch on one's shoulder like parrots, giving off no fiery glow but on the contrary sucking light into themselves?
>
> J.M. Coetzee, *Elizabeth Costello* (2004)

Everywhere, Arendt's work is being republished and talked and written about. We seem to be entering into a period of intense interest in the recovery of her thought in literary and cultural studies, which is characterised by various attempts to make her thought speak to the contemporary geopolitical situation. The interest in Arendt spans the disciplines. I recently heard someone at a philosophy conference make use of Arendt's study of Adolf Eichmann as a frame for a discussion of justice and reconciliation in post-apartheid South Africa. A whole crop of recent studies of Kant's philosophy have sought to fill out Arendt's claims about Kant's political importance (Caygill 1989; Munzel 1999). The issue of evil, which caused such controversy around Arendt's book on Eichmann, is an important topic of public discussion once again, featuring heavily, for example, in the South African novelist J.M. Coetzee's (1940–) recent book *Elizabeth Costello* (2003). There has even been a recent study of Wordsworth that cites *The Origins of Totalitarianism* (Bromwitch 1998). Arendt is everywhere. Why is this? What is driving this renewed engagement with her work? The phenomenon of the current buzz around Arendt's name is interesting and potentially instructive in its own right.

A cynic might argue that it's all just down to the vagaries of academic fashion. A reviewer in the *London Review of Books* recently alluded disparagingly to the 'careerism' of the current 'Arendt industry' (Robin: 18). Research in the humanities always needs paradigms to work with; individual researchers need to feel that they have their finger on the pulse, and that they are in touch with a field of critical and cultural research that is current and alive. The same cynic might then claim that researchers invent the fashion for a particular critical figure in order to show that they are cutting edge. But if this is so, then surely these researchers might have unearthed someone a bit more amenable to our contemporary social and political condition than Hannah Arendt? A number of the core claims mounted by Arendt's work can seem old-fashioned, not to say downright embarrassing. For instance, her claims about the distinction between the public and the private lead her to a view of the human body and of nature as non-cultural spaces that are associated with violence, inarticulacy and slavery. These are difficult claims to square with the ecological consciousness of the early twenty-first century. Arendt's defence of the 'violence' that man does to nature in building a cultural world seems particularly out of sorts with the consciousness of impending ecological catastrophe that defines our times. So too, Arendt sometimes sounds as if she is not far off from advocating women's confinement to the home and the keeping of slaves. These kinds of views would seem to be excessively difficult to square with some of the contemporary interests of gender theory, cultural studies and identity politics.

FEMINISM

For a number of feminist thinkers, in particular, Arendt's work has seemed to be profoundly anti-feminist – even though it invests a great deal of importance in topics such as birth, performativity and the body, which have also been key areas of engagement for feminists. The poet Adrienne Rich (1929–) described the experience of reading *The Human Condition* like this:

> The withholding of women from participation in the *vita activa*, the 'common world', and the connection of this with reproductivity, is something from which

she does not so much turn her eyes as stare straight through unseeing. This "great work" is thus a kind of failure for which masculine ideology has no name, precisely because in terms of that ideology it is successful, at the expense of truths the ideology considers irrelevant. To read such a book, by a woman of large spirit and great erudition, can be painful, because it embodies the tragedy of a female mind nourished on male ideologies.

(Rich 1980: 212)

Could it be that Hannah Arendt wants to exclude women from the 'common world', that she denies them a place at the 'table' because she thought their role in culture conscribed by reproduction? A key feminist slogan of the 1970s and 1980s was 'the personal is the political', but the very fundamentals of Arendt's thought would appear to deny this claim. Some of Arendt's comments on race, and on the civil rights movement in America, also put her in a light from which it seems to be excessively difficult to rescue her. For example, she claims in her essay *On Violence* that the aim of the Black Power movement in its infiltration of American universities in the late 1960s 'was to lower academic standards' (CR: 120). Even more than in her comments on imperialist racism twenty years earlier in *The Origins of Totalitarianism*, such observations must jar with most of us.

PSYCHOANALYSIS

Arendt's rather equivocal attitude towards Marxism, and her marked hostility to psychoanalysis, also make her look out of step with the work of some of the most exciting and urgently relevant critical thinkers today. Psychoanalysis, for Arendt, fatally transgresses the boundary between public and private lives. It makes public the inner, psychic life of the individual and fatally unbalances the relationship between actor and storyteller. Arendt thought this to be particularly true of biographies that speculate on the psychic life of their subject. In the preface to her early biography of a Jewish woman from Enlightenment-period Berlin, Rahel Varnhagen, Arendt wrote:

I have deliberately avoided that modern form of indiscretion in which the writer attempts to penetrate his subject's tricks and aspires to know more than the subject knew about himself or was willing to reveal; what I would call the pseudoscientific apparatuses of depth-psychology, psychoanalysis, graphology, etc., fall into this category of curiosity-seeking.

(RV: 83)

When we are studying someone's life and work, Arendt seems to say, it is not our job to 'diagnose' them, to work out what secret aberration it was that made them tick and to bring it to public attention. Private space must always, for Arendt, be respected – or silenced – lest it bite back and invade the public realm, smothering its freedom with 'domestic' concerns and the violence of the household. Arendt's attack on a 'diagnostic' psycho-biographical analysis is echoed in the work of others of her generation, who also shared her critical attitude towards psychoanalysis. The literary critic Paul de Man, for example, wrote that the common 'misreading' of Jean-Jacques Rousseau 'is almost always accompanied by a tone of intellectual and moral superiority, as if the commentators, in the most favourable of cases, had to apologize or to offer a cure for something that went astray in their author'. For de Man, this type of critic claims to know something about Rousseau 'that Rousseau did not wish to know' (de Man 1983: 112). But Arendt and Paul de Man arguably both take a very prescriptive, instrumental view of what psychoanalysis is capable of achieving. In the case of Arendt, this ends up making her sound at worst archaic and patrician, at best intolerant of 'abnormality' and plain buttoned up.

PUBLIC SPACE

Arendt's defence of the freedom and dignity of the public realm can also seem pretty vacuous. In 1962, the critical theorist Jürgen Habermas published a key study of the public space of modernity, *The Structural Transformation of the Public Sphere*, and claimed Arendt as a significant influence. But Habermas later defined Arendt's account of public space as impossibly formalistic and idealistic:

I want only to indicate the curious perspective that Hannah Arendt adopts: a state which is relieved of the administrative processing of social problems; a politics which is cleansed of socio-economic issues; an institutionalization of public liberty which is independent of the organization of public wealth [...] this path is unimaginable for any modern society.

(Habermas 1977: 15)

The substance of Habermas's criticism of Arendt is that her definition of politics cleansed of any preoccupation with 'social' issues, such as the private welfare of citizens and the management of the economy, is 'elitist', nostalgic for the culture of the ancient Greeks, and simply impractical. Arendt always puts the ills of modernity down to the loss of a public culture, but she is very unspecific about what exactly the having of such a culture would entail. Does family life need to be a despotic condition, ruled by the absolute authority of the father, in order to offset the freedom of the public realm? Would women be allowed to participate in this public culture? And what, exactly, would qualify as an acceptable topic of public debate if anything 'private', including all personal/psychical, economic and social issues are to be banned from public discussion?

Given all of these potential objections to her thought, the question of what it is that is driving the current growth of interest in Arendt in literary and cultural studies seems to be hard to answer. In order to approach this question, perhaps it might make sense to step back for a moment from Arendt's thought and to think about the contemporary cultural and political situation.

A great deal has been written lately about the 'death of theory' and about our being in a 'post-theoretical condition', and the contemporary interest in Arendt's work is undoubtedly happening against this background. Such claims about the death of theory are almost always immediately followed, paradoxically, by the further claim that theory lives on, that it is involved in some peculiar or uncanny form of 'afterlife'. Almost as soon as he declares the death of 'high (i.e. post-structuralist) theory' in his book *After Theory*, Terry Eagleton declares that 'If theory means a reasonably systematic reflection on our guiding assumptions, it remains as indispensable as ever' (Eagleton 2004: 2). What such commentators as Eagleton invariably mean by the 'death of theory' is the end of a particular configuration or imagining of theoretical activity in the humanities, namely, the one which is closely associated with the work of French post-structuralist and postmodern philosophers, Jacques Derrida, Michel Foucault and Jean-François Lyotard the most influential among them. Arendt's work offers a way to pursue theory by other means, since her death coincided, more or less, with the invention of this particular idea of theory in the English-speaking world. Like others of her generation, such as the French existentialist Jean-Paul Sartre (who is also the object of a great deal of contemporary critical attention) Arendt then seems to offer options and possibilities, and crucial paradigms, for continuing theoretical work, and thinking about theoretical issues, from a perspective that is unshackled by post-structuralist and postmodern orthodoxies about, say, the arbitrariness of the signifier, or scepticism towards grand narratives.

REALISM

What comes after postmodernism? In the view of some critics, such as the philosophers Christopher Norris (1947–) and Roy Bhaskar (1944–), the post-postmodern condition can be described as an era of 'critical realism'. Norris's examples for critical realism come from the Anglo-American tradition of analytical philosophy, and in particular from the work of philosophers of science such as Hilary Putnam (1926–) (Norris 2002). But Arendt, too, was committed to an idea of realism. In *The Origins of Totalitarianism* she proposed an 'attentive facing up to, and resisting of, reality – whatever it may be or might have been'. For Arendt, the major characteristic of the totalitarian environment is what she describes as a 'pervasive loss of reality', brought on by a combination of propaganda and the politics of terror. The main symptom of this loss of reality, Arendt argues, is a condition of loneliness, the loss of the sense of connection and connectedness with others which comes from meaningful human speech and interaction. Adolf Eichmann, for example, had lost reality because he was systematically incapable of thinking from someone else's point of view, with distressing and, for Arendt at least, often comic consequences.

Arendt's work then remained committed to defending the real world, and to understanding that world as a space of human togetherness. Arendt wants us to believe that the disturbing tone of *Eichmann in Jerusalem*, its dark comedy and its attentiveness to Eichmann's own conduct of thought – or rather of thoughtlessness – is a product of her own attentive facing up to reality. Those who refused to give up on the view of Eichmann as a figure of radical evil, a conniving liar who tried to dissimulate his evil (and succeeded, they would argue, in pulling the wool over Hannah Arendt's eyes), and those who were shocked and horrified by Arendt's conclusions about Eichmann's banality, were still, in her view, shackled by a metaphysical idea of justice that refused to face up to the full force of totalitarianism's destruction of meaning.

FEELING

Should we really follow Arendt this far? Is there not, after all, something inappropriate, tactless even, about *Eichmann in Jerusalem*, and might this lack of tact gesture towards much deeper problems in Arendt's argument? In a brilliant critique of Arendt's realism, the critical thinker Rei Terada has recently reread *Eichmann in Jerusalem* in light of Freudian ideas of infant psychology, and in particular Freud's theory of 'reality testing'. According to Terada, what Arendt offers in *Eichmann in Jerusalem* is not so much an attentive facing up to reality as a gleeful triumph over it. Terada quotes from a letter that Arendt wrote to her friend the novelist Mary McCarthy in which she confides that she wrote the book 'in a curious state of euphoria' (Terada 2008: 96). Terada argues that both Arendt and Eichmann managed to evade the reality of the totalitarian crimes by failing to admit their real feelings about those crimes. Eichmann told the court repeatedly of his feelings of 'elation' when he advanced his career, and Arendt noted that he still seemed to be elated when he went to the gallows (EJ: 252). In a similar way, Arendt confessed to her friend that she had experienced a feeling of 'euphoria' in writing her book. Terada asks: Why is it that neither Arendt nor Eichmann could admit that the horror they had witnessed or described made them feel terrible? In both instances, a denial of real feelings when faced with horror induces a peculiar transcendence, a feeling of 'elation' or 'euphoria', rather than sorrow or indignation.

Terada's argument restates the accusation levelled at Arendt by Gershom Scholem at the time of the Eichmann controversy, that she had been 'heartless' in her report on the trial (Terada 2008: 96). But it phrases this accusation in a new and theoretically sophisticated way: the defender of authentic human action against the violence inflicted onto it by theory had no space in her own thought for thinking about emotions, least of all her own. Once again, Arendt appears in this reading to be buttoned up and repressed.

Terada's analysis brings a psychoanalytical framework to bear on its reading of Arendt, in order to work both with and against her. Perhaps we need to revisit the view of Arendt as unconditionally hostile to psychoanalysis. While it makes grand dismissive gestures against any attempt to psychologise the phenomenon of totalitarianism, by explaining it, for example, as an emanation of the charisma of the authoritarian personality, *The Origins of Totalitarianism* still proposes an alternative kind of social psychology. We can see this in Arendt's treatment of the complex desire and loathing felt towards Jews in nineteenth-century Paris, and in her treatment of the 'fascination' effect of the imperialist adventurer and the totalitarian leader. One of the most interesting aspects of Arendt's work is the way that it invokes psychological and affective explanations for political phenomena, in order to put them down again, without ever quite succeeding. Arendt remained suspicious of the ways in which a psychological explanation of political and social phenomena assumed a 'hidden meaning' to those phenomena, and in the process risked overlooking what was most overt, public and announced in them. In the case of Eichmann, this meant that she wanted to allow the individual personality – even the non-personality of a man like Eichmann – to speak itself in public, without trying to assume and diagnose something private and hidden that stood behind his words. Arendt thought of storytelling as a useful way to do this. Arendt wants to tell a different kind of public life-story in her account of Eichmann, one that refuses to diagnose symptoms of hidden psychological motivations in the public appearance of Eichmann's (non)-personality in the courtroom, but rather assumes that his cliché-ridden language discloses who Eichmann really was. Her interest in a different form of narrative has been crucially enabling for recent critical thought.

9/11: GRIEF AND NARRATIVE

The attacks on the World Trade Center and the Pentagon on 11 September 2001 undoubtedly amount to a key public event in the life of the new 'post-theoretical theory'. In her book *Precarious Life*, the critical thinker and gender theorist Judith Butler deploys a psycho-analytic framework in order to ask why it was that the events of 9/11 led to 'reactive aggression' against Afghanistan and Iraq (Butler 2004: xiv), and also to think about how those events might have led to a different outcome. What if, Butler asks, the feelings of loss and grief that America and Americans suffered on that day had led them to recognise those feelings as signs of a human condition of 'bodily vulnerability' shared in common with others around the world? What if they had chosen to recognise in their experience of shock, grief and loss, something shared with others who have suffered loss elsewhere, often as a result of American foreign policy, rather than a call for revenge?

What is shared as a common human condition is, for Butler, precisely the bodily condition of being fragile, and vulnerable to the violence of others. Butler argues that such recognition of a common human vulnerability could not take place post-9/11 because there exists no public sphere in which the life-stories of other people who have suffered violence might be heard:

> The public sphere is constituted in part by what cannot be said and what cannot be shown. The limits of the sayable, the limits of what can appear, circumscribe the domain in which political speech operates and certain kinds of subjects appear as viable actors

> (Butler 2004: xvii)

The assumption that public space is dependent upon, and circumscribed by, that which cannot appear in public seems to be highly Arendtian – as does Butler's focus on speech, action and appearance. Yet Butler wants to go further than Arendt, and in particular to test the limits of what can appear in public. The testing out of another public culture would involve, for Butler, an effort to tell the story of 9/11 in a different way. But she is fully aware of how difficult it is to imagine a different way of telling this story that does not simply give in to the view that America 'had it coming' or that it 'got what it deserved'. To 'begin to tell the story a different way, to ask how things came to this', she writes, seems 'already to complicate the question of agency which, no doubt, leads to the fear of moral equivocation'. To avoid this moral equivocation, Butler writes, 'we have to begin the story with the experience of violence we suffered' (Butler 2004: 6). In order for America to sustain its sense of being a victim, it prescribes the kind of agency that it allows to be thought in public. In particular, it limits agency to the perpetrators of the attacks:

> If someone tries to start the story earlier, there are only a few narrative options. We can narrate, for instance, what Mohammed Atta's family life was like, whether he was teased for looking like a girl, where he congregated in Hamburg, and what led, psychologically, to the moment in which he piloted the plane into the World Trade Center.

> (Butler 2004: 5)

The only kind of 'backstory' to 9/11 that is allowed to appear in public involves psychological speculation about the question of what motivated the perpetrators of the attacks. Any attempt to think outside this notion of first-person agency is immediately accused of blurring the moral issues, and excusing the attacks.

Butler wants to imagine a different kind of narrative, one that neither attributes the attacks entirely to the global conditions caused, in part, by American foreign policy (what appears as 'moral equivocation'), nor to attribute them entirely to the sovereign agency of the suicide attackers. She claims instead that to 'take the self-generated acts of the individual as our point of departure in moral reasoning is precisely to foreclose the possibility of questioning what kind of world gives rise to such individuals' (Butler 2004: 16). Rather, this narrative of first-world victimage needs to be reframed in the context of global conditions.

> When President Arroyo of the Philippines on October 29, 2001, remarks that 'the best breeding ground [for terrorism] is poverty,' or Arundhati Roy claims that bin Laden has been 'sculpted from the spare rib of a world laid waste by America's foreign policy,' something less than a strictly causal explanation is being offered […] Indeed, both of them make use of figures – grounds and bones – to bespeak a kind of generation that precedes and exceeds a strictly causal frame. Both of them are pointing to conditions, not causes […] Conditions do not 'act' in the way that individual agents do, but no agent acts without them. They are presupposed in what we do, but it would be a mistake to personify them as if they acted in the place of us.
>
> (Butler 2004: 10–11)

The way that Butler tells the story, the events of 9/11 are neither to be explained as a direct result of the sovereign agency of the terrorists, nor explained away as an automatic outcome of a world of terrible inequality that leads young men to make such radical and violent gestures against that world's dominant power. Rather, Butler wants to show both that those actors owned their acts, and that their acts were partly conditioned by the world into which the actors were born. The power of literary narrative, which sidesteps a causal account of agency, allows Butler (and before her Arundhati Roy and the president of the Philippines) to imagine in a different way the relationship between acts and conditions. Butler wants to rethink our ideas of agency and personal responsibility, in order to suggest that acts for which the individual actor holds full responsibility can still be shown to have been shaped by global conditions. This relationship between act and condition can, she shows, be captured through the figural ground offered by story-telling. As for Arendt's account of the 'crystallisation' of social elements into totalitarianism, for Butler's account of 9/11 it is the power of narrative rather than the causal frame of history that can understand the acts of others in a meaningful way.

BIOPOLITICS AND BARE LIFE

Butler's argument amounts to an attempt to overcome the distinction between what counts as a life that can be grieved over and turned into the subject of a story (the victim of 9/11) and the kind of life that cannot appear in public (the dead Iraqi or Afghani child). Butler's work is one example of a much wider contemporary interest in the juridical understanding and prescription of what life is, and of how such a juridical understanding of life is allied to state power. In his book *Homo Sacer: Sovereign Power and Bare Life* (1995) the Italian poli-tical theorist Giorgio Agamben writes that 'Today politics knows no value (and, consequently, no non-value) other than life' (Agamben 1998: 10). Agamben follows Michel Foucault in naming this political preoccupation with life 'biopolitics'. He argues that Foucault and Arendt were the first to show that 'at the threshold of the modern era, natural life begins to be included in the mechanisms and calcula-tions of State power, and politics turns into *biopolitics*' (Agamben 1998: 3).

Biopolitics, rather like 'political economy', is an oxymoron, splicing together two things that, in the classical political tradition, have been defined as mutually exclusive. Since Aristotle, the sphere of politics has excluded the biological necessities of life included in the Greek term for bare life, *zoē*, from its sphere of public concern. Foucault's notion of biopolitics shows that modernity is instead defined by an erasure of this classical distinction between life and politics, whereby the political realm has become more and more preoccupied with the management of life. Agamben develops Foucault's work on biopolitics by bringing it into dialogue with Arendt's critique of modern society, which had told the story of a progressive incursion of 'nature' into 'culture', culmi-nating in the gas chambers at Auschwitz. Agamben shares in Arendt's critique of the modern world as a space in which the biological life processes of labour and consumerism have come to dominate the political stage, so that politics has conversely redefined its purpose as the protection of those life processes.

Agamben goes even further than Arendt in arguing that the announced preoccupation with the value of life in modern politics belies the way in which politics has, since its very inception, secretly depended on the domination of 'bare life'. According to Agamben, understanding the reality of biopolitics means recognising that the sheer, unmediated physical and natural condition of being alive has always been the central preoccupation of politics, even though politics has claimed, since the time of Aristotle, to separate itself off from this bodily condition. The announced exclusion of 'life' from political interest has then served to render the political status of life unclear. To this extent, the bare life 'dwells in the no-man's-land between the home and the city' (Agamben 1998: 90). This dissolution of the boundary between home and city, *oikos* and *polis*, has had the effect of subjecting 'bare life' directly to sovereign power, unprotected by laws that it seems to stand outside of. This direct confrontation between bare life and sovereignty has meant that the bare life can be destroyed by that sovereign power at any moment.

Agamben's central and paradoxical claim is that a politics which self-consciously holds up the fact of human life as a value, actually gives itself the power to take life away in an utterly arbitrary fashion. He understands the concentration camp as the ultimate site of bio-political power in which this absolute subjection takes place. The camps are, as such, 'the hidden paradigm of the political space of modernity' (Agamben 1998: 123). But according to Agamben, the centrality of the 'bare life' to politics is not limited to totalitarian regimes, but also founds liberal democracy. This means that the kind of experience of the concentration camp victim, which in Arendt's argument is outside or beyond state law in a 'phantom' world of lost reality, for Agamben is the quintessence of law. This is how Agamben ultimately turns Arendt's argument around. The application of law to real human lives is increasingly, for Agamben, an exercise of power understood as sheer domination. As André Duarte claims in a recent essay on Arendt and Agamben, 'When politics is conceived of as bio-politics, as the task of increasing the life and happiness of the national *animal laborans* [man-as-labouring-animal], the nation-state becomes [...] violent and murderous' (King and Stone 2007: 198).

Agamben fills out the logic in Arendt's different arguments and, in particular, he brings together the arguments of *The Human Condition* and *The Origins of Totalitarianism*. One example of the bare life is the newborn, who for Arendt figures the possibility of a new beginning, the founding of a new politics of action based in freedom. For Agamben, conversely, the newborn is instead a figure of raw, absolutely vulnerable humanity stripped of all rights and exposed to sovereign power. The newborn is a figure that seems to be exceptional in the way that she stands outside the law, or at the threshold of the law, but she is in fact the archetypal political subject, vulnerable and subjected to the unmediated power of a violent political sovereignty. In a different way, the concentration camp is, in Agamben's argument, the most absolute biopolitical space that has ever been realised – a space in which power confronts pure biological life without any mediation. At times in *The Origins of Totalitarianism* Arendt entertained the idea, popular among other critical theorists, that liberal democracy is basically just a different form of totalitarianism. At one point, for example, she compares techniques of advertising to the propaganda techniques of totalitarian regimes (OT3: 43). But Arendt was never prepared to follow these suggestions through, partly because they seem to her excessively to psychologise the phenomenon of totalitarianism, and partly out of her loyalty to the founding principles of liberal democracy as they were practised in the American revolution and laid down in the American constitution. But Agamben fills out this logic, claiming the concentration camp as an inversion of the human condition in a '*conditio inhumana*'.

ETHICS

Where Arendt understands totalitarianism as a 'subterranean stream of European history' (OT1: xi), an aberration from the tradition of Western politics, for Agamben the logic of the Nazi biopolitical regime has been in the Western tradition all along. We need this kind of reading with Arendt and against her more than ever, since contemporary biopolitical phenomena such as the US prison at Guantánamo Bay show that the assault of sovereign states on 'bare life' is indeed the rule rather than the exception. Another widening of Arendt's critique in order to take in all of liberal democracy is found in Slavoj Žižek's recent book *Violence* (2008). In particular, Žižek offers a productive inversion of

Arendt's understanding of storytelling as a meaningful disclosure of action. In his book, Žižek inverts the binary opposition between inside and outside, public and private that guides Arendt's thought. For Arendt, the public manifestation of the self in storytelling constitutes its real meaning, rather than that self's inner understanding of itself; this is the reason why she was so hostile to psychoanalysis. According to Žižek, on the contrary, the stories we tell about ourselves instead show our infinite capacity for self-deception. He describes a memoir written by the son of Lavrenty Beria, one of Stalin's co-workers, 'presenting his father as a warm family man who simply followed Stalin's orders and secretly tried to limit the damage'.

> The experience that we have of our lives from within, the story we tell ourselves about ourselves, in order to account for what we are doing, is fundamentally a lie – the truth lies outside, in what we do.
>
> (Žižek 2008: 40)

The claim here is of a divorce between storytelling and the meaning of action. Žižek does not locate this divorce solely in the 'exception' of the Holocaust and totalitarianism, but understands it as a central principle of liberal democracy. In a liberal society, for Žižek, the story we tell ourselves about ourselves is that we are tolerant and liberal, but the reality of our contemporary geopolitical experience is that we are violently hostile to any 'other' who may not be the way we desire him to be – the object of our benevolence and tolerance. We are all, in a sense, potential (or real) 'Eichmenn'. Žižek asks, 'What if […] such a blindness, such a violent exclusionary gesture of refusing to see, such a disavowal of reality […] is the innermost constituent of *every* ethical stance?' (Žižek 2008: 44). According to this argument, acting in society requires that we forget about the ethical reality that underpins our actions – none of us, argues Žižek, could eat a pork chop if we knew what goes on in the abattoir. Far from being a defining characteristic of totalitarianism, such a failure of reality is, for Žižek, the defining characteristic of any so-called liberal society.

The most interesting work after Arendt uses her to rethink ethical norms in a (post)-totalitarian world. These efforts involve thinking in particular about the question of the real in relation to our ideas of ourselves as ethical and affective beings. For critical thinkers since Arendt, violence is not, as she had argued, distinct from power, its private face, and an aberration from the political, but the core essence of liberal politics in the West. My point is that such critiques work with and against Arendt. They radicalise her to a point that she was unwilling to go to in her appreciation for certain aspects of the Western liberal political tradition, but equally, they could never have got as far as they do without her. Agamben writes that Arendt's work 'remains, even today, practically without continuation' (Agamben 1998: 4) and that only by looking at the structural centrality of the bare life to our political experience will it become possible 'to clear the way for the new politics, which remains largely to be invented' (Agamben 1998: 11). This might be construed as a radicalisation of something that had been implicit in Arendt but that she hadn't wanted to face up to – but the call for a new politics, the claim that politics cannot exist until we get past the experience of the concentration camps and what they represent, is crucially enabled by Arendt.

Arendt is an indispensable figure for our current political crisis, the new dark times that we are living through in which bare life is being brutalised around the globe in increasingly disturbing and strangely public forms. Her call for a new politics has seldom seemed more urgent.

FURTHER READING

WORKS BY HANNAH ARENDT

INTRODUCTORY

Arendt, Hannah (1983) *Men in Dark Times,* San Diego, CA and New York: Harcourt Brace & Co.

This book of essays about key figures of the twentieth century shows Arendt at her most incisive, insightful and accessible.

Arendt, Hannah (2006) 'What is Freedom?' and 'What is Authority?', in Jerome Kohn (ed.) *Between Past and Future: Eight Exercises in Political Thought*, London: Penguin.

Although they are both very dense, these essays give a short way in to key concepts in Arendt's thought that will help to give a general sense of its overall scope. 'What is Authority?' is particularly useful for thinking about Arendt's fundamental approach to politics, as we see her here refuse what she understands to be a false choice between left and right politics.

Arendt, Hannah (2004) 'On the Nature of Totalitarianism: An Essay in Understanding', in Jerome Kohn (ed.) *Essays in Understanding 1930–1954: Formation, Exile and Totalitarianism*, New York: Schocken Books.

Arendt was a prolific writer of journalism, and while there are several key texts that every Arendt scholar needs to tackle at some point (see below), her occasional pieces are often excellent and accessible. *Essays in Understanding* was the first of four new editions of previous uncollected and untranslated essays by Arendt that have been recently published by Schocken Books, all edited by Jerome Kohn, which together provide an excellent resource for anyone looking to find their way around Arendt's work for the first time. They are extensive, relatively cheap, well presented and organised under useful thematic headings. The other editions are as follows.

Arendt, Hannah, ed. Jerome Kohn (2005) *Responsibility and Judgment*, New York: Schocken Books.

Arendt, Hannah, ed. Jerome Kohn (2007) *The Promise of Politics*, New York: Schocken Books.

Arendt, Hannah, ed. Jerome Kohn and Ron H. Feldman (2007) *The Jewish Writings*, New York: Schocken Books.

ARENDT AS LITERARY CRITIC

Arendt, Hannah, ed. Susannah Young-Ah Gottlieb (2007) *Reflections on Literature and Culture,* Stanford: Stanford University Press.

This book usefully brings together all of Arendt's writings on literature and culture, comprising both essays and excerpts from the longer texts. These are organised chronologically, and show the consistency of Arendt's thoughts about art across her thinking career. It also has an excellent introductory essay on Arendt's view of artistic culture.

MAJOR WORKS

Arendt, Hannah, ed. Ronald Beiner (1982) *Lectures on Kant's Political Philosophy,* Chicago: University of Chicago Press.

Arendt, Hannah (1998) *The Human Condition*, Chicago: University of Chicago Press.

Arendt, Hannah, ed. Samantha Power (2006) *The Origins of Totalitarianism*, New York: Schocken Books.

This is the most up-to-date, single-volume edition of this early classic text of Arendt's. Power's introduction tries to relate Arendt's theory of totalitarianism to the contemporary 'war on terror'.

These three are Arendt's most often-cited works. They fit together to tell the story of modernity, as Arendt understood it. The Chicago edition of Arendt's Kant lectures also includes a really useful interpretative essay by the editor Ronald Beiner, which is particularly strong on the connections between Arendt's treatment of totalitarianism and Kant's theory of judgement.

Arendt, Hannah (1994) *Eichmann in Jerusalem: A Report on the Banality of Evil*, Harmondsworth: Penguin.

Arendt's best known and most controversial work.

CORRESPONDENCE

Arendt, Hannah, ed. Carol Brightman (1995) *Between Friends: The Correspondence of Hannah Arendt and Mary McCarthy 1949–1975*, London: Secker & Warburg.

Arendt, Hannah, ed. Ursula Ludz (2003) *Letters: 1925–1975, Hannah Arendt and Martin Heidegger*, New York: Harcourt.

These volumes of letters undoubtedly give a rich contextualisation of Arendt in her life and times.

WORKS ON HANNAH ARENDT

INTRODUCTORY

Benhabib, Seyla   (1996) *The Reluctant Modernism of Hannah Arendt*, London and New Delhi: Sage.

Benhabib privileges OT over HC as the core Arendt text. She seeks to reconcile Arendt's thought to Habermas, and generally to argue that we should not take Arendt's critical view of society at face value. The book also has a very insightful chapter on Arendt and Heidegger. It already seems a bit dated in the way that it wants to defend the state of Israel against Arendt's attacks on it. In the ten or so years since Benhabib's book came out, Arendt's treatment of Israel has come to look more and more prescient. The book also has an excellent chapter on Arendt and storytelling, which works with her essay on Walter Benjamin from MDT.

Canovan, Margaret (1992) *Hannah Arendt: A Reinterpretation of Her Political Thought*, Cambridge: Cambridge University Press.

Canovan works extensively with archival material, and particularly a manuscript on Karl Marx, in order to show the links between OT and HC, and in particular the ways that each presupposes the arguments of the other. Generally a hugely scholarly and well thought out account of Arendt, and probably the best single introduction to her thought that there is.

Young-Bruehl, Elisabeth (2006) *Why Arendt Matters*, New Haven and London: Yale University Press.
Makes some interesting comments on Arendt's treatment of forgiveness in relation to the Truth and Reconciliation Commission in South Africa, but this is a book which is a bit light on detailed engagement with her texts and which draws some rather questionable analogies between twentieth-century totalitarianism and al-Qaeda.

BIOGRAPHIES

Kristeva, Julia (2001) *Hannah Arendt*, trans. Ross Guberman, New York: Columbia University Press.
This is the first of three biographies published by the famous French feminist in her series *Female Genius: Life, Madness, Words*. It's interesting to see what a feminist and psychoanalyst makes of Arendt, given Arendt's hostility to both psychoanalysis and feminism! Kristeva has some trouble squaring her idea of genius with Arendt's, for whom the idea is very individualistic and Romantic. Nevertheless, the early part of her study is focused on Arendt's ideas about narrative, and Kristeva brings some very interesting observations to that area of Arendt's thought.

Young-Bruehl, Elisabeth (2004) *Hannah Arendt: For the Love of the World* (2nd edn), New Haven and London: Yale University Press.
The definitive biography of Arendt. Dense and rewarding, it is as insightful on Arendt's life-story as it is on her ideas. The author was one of the first to gain access to Arendt's private papers, and when the biography was first published in 1982, it told for the first time in public the story of Arendt's affair with Heidegger.

COLLECTIONS OF ESSAYS

Hill, Melvyn (ed.) (1979) *Hannah Arendt: Recovery of the Public World*, New York: St Martin's Press.

The oldest – and in some ways the best – collection of essays on Arendt, which were put together while she was still alive and before the publication of LM and LKPP. Has excellent essays on Arendt's relation to Marx and her use of storytelling, and generally forwards a very strong argument for Arendt's independence from other 'schools' of critical thought.

Honig, Bonnie (ed.) (1995) *Feminist Interpretations of Hannah Arendt*, University Park: Penn State University Press.

Although Arendt's relationship with feminism was often fractious, this collection of essays marks the attempt to use some of her key ideas – for example, labour, natality and performativity, to actively enable a feminist politics. This happens with varying degrees of success in the different essays. The book includes a useful annotated bibliography of feminist engagements with Arendt.

King, Richard H. and Stone, Dan (eds) (2007) *Hannah Arendt and the Uses of History: Imperialism, Nation, Race and Genocide*, New York and Oxford: Berghahn Books.

A new collection of essays which seeks to shift readings of Arendt away from political philosophy towards a focus on her as an historian. A number of engagements with OT contest certain aspects of her thought in ingenious ways – i.e. by using her to think about the Yugoslav wars of the 1990s. The series introduction, and several of the essays, usefully position Arendt in relation to the work of contemporaries who are often ignored by more 'straight' political philosophy readings of her – i.e. Aimé Césaire and Emmanuel Levinas. Many of the essays take Arendt's work as a springboard to think about the contemporary global situation – to this extent they constitute more of a use of Arendt than a close exposition of her ideas.

Villa, Dana (ed.) (2002) *The Cambridge Companion to Hannah Arendt*, Cambridge: Cambridge University Press.

Offers a usefully clear selection of essays on different areas of Arendt's thought such as judgement, totalitarianism, freedom and politics, by a number of established scholars in the field.

LITERARY CRITICISM

Cavarrero, Adriana (2000) *Relating Narratives: Storytelling and Selfhood*, trans. Paul A. Kottman, London: Routledge.

This is the first study from the perspective of narrative theory to offer a really sustained application of Arendt's concept of storytelling.

Wilkinson, Lynn R. (2004) 'Hannah Arendt and Isak Dinesen: Between Storytelling and Theory', *Comparative Literature* 56(1): 77–98.
A useful article on Arendt's theory of storytelling.

STUDIES OF ARENDT'S POLITICAL THOUGHT

Bernstein, Richard J. (1996) *Hannah Arendt and the Jewish Question*, Cambridge: Polity Press.
Makes the argument that all of Arendt's major political ideas can be traced back to her political experiences as a Jew and her early thinking about the 'Jewish question'.

Disch, Lisa (1996) *Hannah Arendt and the Limits of Philosophy*, Ithaca: Cornell University Press.
Generally very good on the ethical dimensions of Arendt's theory of action (friendship and forgiveness), and has lots on the role of story-telling in establishing a 'truthful' standpoint which is involved in the plural world of human affairs, rather than standing back from it.

Passerin d'Entrèves, Maurizio (1994) *The Political Philosophy of Hannah Arendt*, London and New York: Routledge.
A really excellent and clear introduction to Arendt's political thought, with useful chapters on topics such as action and judgement. The book emphasises the democratic elements of Arendt's work against criticism of her elitism, and has a few very good pages on storytelling.

Kateb, George (1984) *Hannah Arendt: Politics, Conscience, Evil*, Oxford: Martin Robertson.
An exhaustive and at times exhausting enquiry into Arendt's theory of political action. Puts forward the rather controversial thesis that there exists a symmetry between Arendt's argument and totalitarian ideology.

Parekh, Bikhu (1981) *Hannah Arendt and the Search for a New Political Philosophy*, Basingstoke: Macmillan.
Gives a good overview of Arendt's relation to political philosophy, and a summary of the phenomenological background and its impact on her. Can be a bit repetitive and tends to abstract the particular

arguments from their contexts. Nevertheless, essential reading for anyone approaching Arendt from the viewpoint of political theory.

Villa, Dana (1995) *Arendt and Heidegger: The Fate of the Political*, Princeton: Princeton University Press.

Exhasutive study which makes for essential reading for anyone interested in the relation between Arendt and Heidegger's thought. This relation only takes up the second half of the book. The first half is as informative about her relation to the thought of Aristotle, as Villa wants to prise Arendt free from the claim (mounted by Habermas and others) that she is a 'neo-Aristotelian'.

JOURNALS

Hannah Arendt Newsletter
Sometimes contains articles by philosophers and theorists such as Jonathan Rée reflecting on her work. See below for a web link.

There have been four editions of the journal *Social Research* dedicated to Arendt's work; in 1977, shortly after her death (44(1)); in 1990 (57(1)); in 2002 (69(2)), commemorating the fiftieth anniversary of the publication of OT; and the most recent marking the centenary of Arendt's birth in 2007 in two separate parts (74(3/4)). All contain invaluable articles by established Arendt scholars.

OTHER

Lyotard, Jean-François (1993) 'The Survivor', in Robert Harvey and Mark S. Roberts (eds), *Toward the Postmodern*, New Jersey: Humanities Press.

An opportunity to read the most celebrated postmodern philosopher thinking about Arendt and the Holocaust.

WEBSITES

www.Hannaharendt.net
A useful website that lists all the new material appearing on Arendt, and reviews conferences on her work. Contains a link to the web-based *Hannah Arendt Newsletter* (see above) and even lists a series of interviews with Arendt that, at the time of going to press, can be watched on YouTube (in French).

www.youtube.com

WORKS CITED

Original dates of publication are given in square brackets where appropriate.

Adorno, Theodor (2003 [1951]) 'Cultural Criticism and Society', in Neil Levi and Michael Rothberg (eds) *The Holocaust: Theoretical Readings*, New Brunswick: Rutgers University Press, pp. 280–81.

Agamben, Giorgio (1998) *Homo Sacer: Sovereign Power and Bare Life*, trans. Daniel Heller-Roazen, Stanford: Stanford University Press.

Althusser, Louis (2001 [1969]) 'Ideology and Ideological State Apparatus (Notes Towards an Investigation)', in *Lenin and Philosophy and Other Essays*, trans. Ben Brewster, New York: Monthly Review Press, pp. 85–126.

Arendt, Hannah (1972) *Crises of the Republic*, Harmondsworth: Penguin.

—— (1981 [1971]) *The Life of the Mind*, San Diego, CA and New York: Harcourt Brace.

—— (1983) *Men in Dark Times*, San Diego, CA and New York: Harcourt Brace.

—— (1985 [1951]) *The Origins of Totalitarianism*, 3 vols, San Diego, CA and New York: Harcourt Brace.

—— (1990 [1963]) *On Revolution*, Harmondsworth: Penguin.

— (1990) 'Philosophy and Politics', *Social Research* 57:1, pp. 73–103.

— (1992) *Lectures on Kant's Political Philosophy*, Ronald Beiner (ed.), Chicago: University of Chicago Press.

— (1994 [1963]) *Eichmann in Jerusalem: A Report on the Banality of Evil*, Harmondsworth: Penguin.

— (1997) *Rahel Varnhagen: The Life of a Jewess*, Liliane Weissberg (ed.), Baltimore and London: Johns Hopkins University Press.

— (1998 [1958]) *The Human Condition*, Chicago: University of Chicago Press.

— (2005) *Essays in Understanding 1930–1954: Formation, Exile, and Totalitarianism*, Jerome Kohn (ed.), New York: Schocken Books.

— (2006) *Between Past and Future: Eight Exercises in Political Thought*, Jerome Kohn (ed.), London: Penguin.

— (2006 [1951]) *The Origins of Totalitarianism*, Samantha Power (ed.), New York: Schocken Books.

— (2007a) *The Jewish Writings*, Jerome Kohn and Ron H. Feldman (eds), New York: Schocken Books.

— (2007b) *Reflections on Literature and Culture*, Susannah Young-Ah Gottlieb (ed.), Stanford: Stanford University Press.

Barthes, Roland (2001 [1967]) 'The Death of the Author', in Vincent B. Leitch et al. (eds), *The Norton Anthology of Theory and Criticism*, New York, London: W.W. Norton & Co, pp. 1466–70.

Benhabib, Seyla (1996) *The Reluctant Modernism of Hannah Arendt*, London, New Delhi: Sage

Benjamin, Walter (1992 [1950]) 'Theses on the Philosophy of History', in Hannah Arendt (ed.) *Illuminations*, London: Fontana, pp. 245–55.

Bernstein, Richard J. (1996) *Hannah Arendt and the Jewish Question*, Cambridge: Polity Press.

Bromwitch, David (1998) *Disowned by Memory: Wordsworth's Poetry of the 1790s*, Chicago and London: University of Chicago Press.

Burke, Edmund (1999 [1790]) *Reflections on the Revolution in France*, in Isaac Kramnick (ed.), *The Portable Edmund Burke*, London: Penguin.

Butler, Judith (2004) *Precarious Life: The Powers of Mourning and Violence*, London and New York: Verso.

Canovan, Margaret (1992) *Hannah Arendt: A Reinterpretation of Her Political Thought*, Cambridge: Cambridge University Press.

Carey, John (1992) *The Intellectuals and the Masses: Pride and Prejudice among the Literary Intelligentsia, 1880–1939*, London: Faber and Faber.

Caygill, Howard (1989) *Art of Judgement*, Oxford: Basil Blackwell.

Ceserani, David (2007) *Becoming Eichmann: Rethinking the Life, Crimes and Trial of a Desk Murderer*, New York, Cambridge MA: Da Capo Press.

Chrisman, Laura and Williams, Patrick (eds) (1994) *Colonial Discourse and Post-Colonial Theory: A Reader*, New York: Columbia University Press.

Coetzee, J.M. (2004) *Elizabeth Costello*, London: Vintage.

Conrad, Joseph (2000 [1902]) *Heart of Darkness*, Robert Hampson (ed.), London: Penguin.

de Man, Paul (1983) *Blindness and Insight: Essays in the Rhetoric of Contemporary Criticism* (2nd edn), Wlad Godrich (ed.), London: Routledge.

Derrida, Jacques (1978) 'Structure, Sign and Play in the Discourse of the Human Sciences', in *Writing and Difference,* trans. Alan Bass, London: Routledge.

Duarte, André (2007) 'Hannah Arendt, Biopolitics, and the Problem of Violence', in Richard H. King and Dan Stone (eds), *Hannah Arendt and the Uses of History: Imperialism, Nation, Race, and Genocide,* New York and Oxford: Berghahn Books, pp. 191–204.

Eagleton, Terry (1990) *The Ideology of the Aesthetic*, Oxford: Blackwell.

— (2004) *After Theory*, London: Penguin.

Eliot, T.S. (1990 [1922]) 'The Waste Land', in *The Waste Land and Other Poems*, London: Faber.

Fanon, Frantz (1991 [1951]) *Black Skin/White Masks*, London: Pluto Press.

Foucault, Michel (1980) *Power/Knowledge: Selected Interviews and Other Writings 1972–1977*, Colin Gordon (ed.), Brighton: Harvester.

Habermas, Jürgen (1977) 'Hannah Arendt's Communications Concept of Power', *Social Research* 44(1): 3–24.

Heidegger, Martin (1967 [1927]) *Being and Time*, trans. John Macquarrie and Edward Robinson, Oxford: Basil Blackwell.

— (1993 [1950]) 'The Origin of the Work of Art', in David Farrell Krell (ed.) *Basic Writings: Martin Heidegger*, London: Routledge.

Hinchman, L.P. and Hinchman, S.K. (1984) 'In Heidegger's Shadow: Hannah Arendt's Phenomenological Humanism', *Review of Politics* 46: 183–211.

Joyce, James (1996 [1916]) *A Portrait of the Artist as a Young Man*, London: Penguin.

— (1998 [1922]) *Ulysses*, Jeri Johnson (ed.), London: Penguin.

Kant, Immanuel (1987 [1790]) *Critique of Judgement*, Werner S. Pluhar (ed.), Indianapolis: Hackett Publishing Co.

Kateb, George (1984) *Hannah Arendt: Politics, Conscience, Evil*, Oxford: Martin Robertson.

Kohn, Jerome (2002) 'Arendt's Concept and Description of Totalitarianism', *Social Research* 69(2): 621–56.

Levi, Primo (1987 [1947]) *If This is a Man; The Truce*, trans. Stuart Woolf, London: Abacus.

McGann, Jerome (1983) *The Romantic Ideology: A Critical Investigation*, Chicago: University of Chicago Press.

— (1987) *Social Values and Poetic Acts: The Historical Judgment of Literary Work*, Cambridge, MA: Harvard University Press.

Marx, Karl (1963 [1852]) *The Eighteenth Brumaire of Louis Bonaparte*, New York: International Publishers.

— (1997 [1843]) 'On the Jewish Question', in Loyd D. Easton and Kurt H. Guddat (eds), *Writings of the Young Marx on Philosophy and Society*, Indianapolis and London: Hackett Publishing Co.

Melville, Herman (1993) *Billy Budd and Other Stories*, Robert Lee (ed.), London, Vermont: Everyman.

Munzel, G. Felicitas (1999) *Kant's Conception of Moral Character: The "Critical" Link of Morality, Anthropology, and Reflective Judgment*, Chicago: University of Chicago Press.

Norris, Christopher (2002) *Hilary Putnam: Realism, Reason and the Uses of Uncertainty*, Manchester: Manchester University Press.

Orwell, George (1983 [1949]) *1984*, in *The Penguin Complete Novels of George Orwell*, Harmondsworth: Penguin.

— (2003 [1946]) 'The Prevention of Literature', in *Shooting an Elephant and Other Essays*, London: Penguin.

Plato (1991) *The Republic* (2nd edn), Allan Bloom (ed.), New York: Basic Books.

Rich, Adrienne (1980) *On Lies, Secrets and Silence: Selected Prose 1966–1978*, London: Virago.

Robin, Corey (2007) 'Dragon Slayers', *London Review of Books*, 4 January: 18–20.

Rousseau, Jean-Jacques (1987 [1762]) *On the Social Contract*, trans. Donald A. Cress, Indianapolis: Hackett Publishing Co.

Said, Edward (1993) *Culture and Imperialism*, London: Chatto & Windus.

Sebald, W.G. (2001) *Austerlitz*, London: Penguin.

Stein, Gertrud (1922) 'Sacred Emily', in *Geography and Plays*, Boston: The Four Seas Company.

Terada, Rei (2008) 'Thinking for Oneself: Realism and Defiance in Arendt', *Textual Practice* 22(1): 85–111.

Villa, Dana (1996) *Arendt and Heidegger: The Fate of the Political*, Princeton: Princeton University Press.

Woolf, Virginia (2000 [1925]) *Mrs Dalloway*, Elaine Showalter (ed.), Penguin: London.

Wordsworth, William (1963 [1802]) 'Preface to *Lyrical Ballads*', in William Wordsworth and S.T. Coleridge, *Lyrical Ballads*, R.L. Brett and A.L. Jones (eds), London: Methuen.

— (1970 [1805]) *The Prelude: The 1805 Text*, Ernest de Selincourt (ed.), Oxford: Oxford University Press.

Young-Bruehl, Elisabeth (2004) *Hannah Arendt: For Love of the World* (2nd edn), New Haven, CT and London: Yale University Press.

— (2006) *Why Arendt Matters*, New Haven, CT: Yale University Press.

Žižek, Slavoj (2008) *Violence*, London: Profile Books.

INDEX

Related titles from Routledge

Theodor Adorno

Ross Wilson

The range of Theodor Adorno's achievement and the depth of his insights are breathtaking and daunting. His work on literary, artistic and musical forms, his devastating indictment of modern industrial society, and his profound grasp of Western culture from Homer to Hollywood have made him one of the most significant figures in twentieth-century thought.

As one of the main philosophers of the Frankfurt School of Critical Theory, Adorno's influence on literary theory, cultural studies and philosophical aesthetics has been immense. His wide-ranging authorship is significant also to continental philosophy, political theory, art criticism and musicology. Key ideas discussed in this guide include:

- art and aesthetics
- fun and free time
- nature and reason
- things, thought and being right

This *Routledge Critical Thinkers* guide will equip readers with the tools required to interpret critically Adorno's major works, while also introducing them to his interpretation of classical German philosophy and his relationship to the most significant of his contemporaries.

ISBN10: 0-415-41818-6 (hbk)
ISBN10: 0-415-41819-4 (pbk)
ISBN10: 0-203-93332-X (ebk)

ISBN13: 978-0-415-41818-8 (hbk)
ISBN13: 978-0-415-41819-5 (pbk)
ISBN13: 978-0-203-93332-9 (ebk)

Available at all good bookshops
For ordering and further information please visit:
www.routledge.com

Stuart Hall

James Procter

Stuart Hall is one of the founding figures of cultural studies. He was director of the Centre for Contemporary Cultural Studies, famously coined the term 'Thatcherrism', and assessed new Labour as the 'great moving nowhere show'. One of the leading public intellectuals of the postwar period, he has helped transform our understanding of culture as both a theoretical category and a political practice. James Procter's introduction places Hall's work within its historical contexts, providing a clear guide to his key ideas and influences, as well as to his critics and his intellectual legacy, covering topics such as

- Popular culture and youth subcultures
- The CCCS and cultural studies
- Media and communication
- Racism and resistance
- Thatcherism
- Identity, ethnicity, diaspora

Stuart Hall is the ideal gateway to the work of a critic described by Terry Eagleton as 'a walking chronicle of everything from the New Left to New Times, Leavis to Lyotard, Aldermaston to ethnicity'.

ISBN10: 0-415-26266-6 (hbk)
ISBN10: 0-415-26267-4 (pbk)

ISBN13: 978-0-415-26266-8 (hbk)
ISBN13: 978-0-415-26267-5 (pbk)
ISBN13: 978-0-203-49698-5 (ebk)

Related titles from Routledge

Slavoj Žižek

Tony Myers

Slavoj Žižek is no ordinary thinker. Combining psychoanalysis, philosophy and politics into a compelling whole, Žižek's approach is always both fresh and fascinating. The scope of his subject matter is equally exhilarating, ranging from political apathy of contemporary life, to a joke about the man who thins he will be eaten by a chicken, from the ethical heroism of Keanu Reeves in 'Speed', to what toilet designs reveal about the national psyche. In this volume, Tony Myers provides a clear and engaging guide to Žižek's key ideas, explaining the main influences on Žižek's thought, most crucially his engagement with Lacanian psychoanalysis, using examples drawn from popular culture and everyday life, Myers outlines for the first time the main issues that Žižek's work tackles, including:

- What is a subject and why is it so important?
- What is so terrible about postmodernity?
- How can we distinguish reality from idealogy?
- What is the relationship between men and women?
- Why is racism always a fantasy?

Slavoj Žižek is essential reading for anyone wanting to understand the thought of the critic whom Terry Eagleton has described as 'the most formidably brilliant exponent of psychoanalysis, indeed of cultural theory in general, to have emerged in Europe for some decades'.

ISBN10: 0-415-26264-X (hbk)
ISBN10: 0-415-26265-8 (pbk)

ISBN13: 978-0-415-26264-4 (hbk)
ISBN13: 978-0-415-26265-1 (pbk)
ISBN13: 978-0-203-63440-0 (ebk)

Available at all good bookshops
For ordering and further information please visit:
www.routledge.com

THE NEW CRITICAL IDIOM

Series Editor: John Drakakis, University of Stirling

The New Critical Idiom is an invaluable series of introductory guides to today's critical terminology. Each book:

- provides a handy, explanatory guide to the use (and abuse) of the term
- offers an original and distinctive overview by a leading literary and cultural critic
- relates the term to the larger field of cultural representation

With a strong emphasis on clarity, lively debate and the widest possible breadth of examples, *The New Critical Idiom* is an indispensable approach to key topics in literary studies.

Available in this series:

For further information on individual books in the series, visit: www.routledgeliterature.com

Related titles from Routledge

Cyberculture Theorists
David Bell

This book surveys a 'cluster' of works that seek to explore the
cultures of cyberspace, the Internet and the information society. It
introduces key ideas, and includes detailed discussion of the work
of two key thinkers in this area, Manuel Castells and Donna Haraway,
as well as outlining the development of cyberculture studies as a
field. To do this, the book also explores selected 'moments' in this
development, from the early 1990s, when cyberspace and cyberculture were only just beginning to come together as ideas, up to
the present day, when the field of cyberculture studies has grown
and bloomed, producing innovative theoretical and empirical work
from a diversity of standpoints. Key topics include:

- Life on the screen
- Network society
- Space of flows
- Cyborg methods

Cyberculture Theorists is the ideal starting point for anyone wanting to
understand how to theorise cyberculture in all its myriad forms.

ISBN10: 0-415-32430-0 (hbk)
ISBN10: 0-415-32431-9 (pbk)
ISBN10: 0-203-35701-9 (ebk)

ISBN13: 978-0-415-32430-4 (hbk)
ISBN13: 978-0-415-32431-1 (pbk)
ISBN13: 978-0-203-35701-9 (ebk)

Related titles from Routledge

Feminist Film Theorists

Shohini Chaudhuri

Since it began in the 1970s, feminist film theory has revolutionized the way that films and their spectators can be understood. This book focuses on the groundbreaking work of Laura Mulvey, Kaja Silverman, Teresa de Lauretis, and Barbara Creed. Each of these thinkers has opened up a new and distinctive approach to the study of film and this book provides the most detailed account so far of their ideas. It illuminates the following six key concepts and demonstrates their value as tools for film analysis:

- the male gaze
- the female voice
- technologies of gender
- queering desire
- the monstrous-feminine
- masculinity in crisis

Shohini Chaudhuri shows how these four thinkers construct their theories through their reading of films as well as testing their ideas with a number of other examples from contemporary cinema and television. She concludes that the concepts have not remained static over the past thirty years but have continually evolved with the influence of new critical debates and developments in film production, signalling their continuing impact and relevance in an era that is often unthinkingly branded as 'post-feminist'.

ISBN10: 0-415-32432-7 (hbk)
ISBN10: 0-415-32433-5 (pbk)
ISBN10: 0-203-35702-7 (ebk)

ISBN13: 978-0-415-32432-8 (hbk)
ISBN13: 978-0-415-32433-5 (pbk)
ISBN13: 978-0-203-35702-6 (ebk)

Available at all good bookshops
For ordering and further information please visit:
www.routledge.com

Literary Theory: The Basics
Third Edition
Hans Bertens

With a new introduction and fully updated pointers to further reading, this third edition of Hans Bertens' bestselling book is a must-have guide to the world of literary theory.

Exploring a broad range of topics from Marxist and feminist criticism to post-modernism and new historicism it includes new coverage of:

- the latest developments in post-colonial and cultural theory
- literature and sexuality
- the latest schools of thought, including eco-criticism and post-humanism
- the future of literary theory and criticism.

Literary Theory: The Basics is an essential purchase for anyone who wants to know what literary theory is and where it is going.

ISBN 13: 978- 0-415-39670-7 (hbk)
ISBN 13: 978- 0-415-39671-4 (pbk)